.

Stop The Storms

Hot Rain

P. J. Naughton

Dedicated to Kathy.

Contents

1. Introduction.

We currently face a major threat to our ongoing survival. Our planet is undergoing a rapid transformation, one which has been brought about largely as a direct result of human activity. Over the last two hundred years or so, fossil fuels have been burned on a massive scale. This has resulted in damage to our climate which is now suffering rapid global warming.

Our planet is constantly bathed in light from the sun. This light brings with it a significant amount of essential heat energy which warms the Earth's surface. Sunlight of course is a vital element to ensure our ongoing survival; it is the essence of life. Not only does it bring light and warmth, it is also essential for growing crops and for fuelling our weather systems. Without it, our planet would rapidly freeze over, mass extinction would occur and possibly all forms of life on Earth would end.

In turn, the Earth radiates heat back out into space but the so called 'greenhouse' gases (GHG) which reside in the atmosphere, effectively form a blanket which traps an increasing amount of this re-radiated energy. These gases help maintain our global temperature, without them our climate would be much cooler, but increased emissions are causing our global temperature to rise and this is leading to catastrophic consequences. There are a number of greenhouse gases, some of the most significant are carbon deposits such as carbon dioxide and methane. Other GHG gases also have a significant impact such as nitrous oxide and even water vapour. It's estimated that in the last two hundred years, the amount of carbon dioxide in our atmosphere has increased by about 50% [1]. The result of the increasing level of greenhouse gases is that our global temperature is now increasing by about 0.2°c per decade. This might not sound like much, but the resulting effects are very significant indeed.

Over recent decades, we have seen a massive increase in violent storms, huge hurricanes and powerful tornadoes. Many of these storms have brought with them a colossal amount of devastation with the loss of thousands of lives, widescale injury and the destruction of homes and other property and infrastructure on a prodigious scale. In addition, thousands of people die each year from the increase in

1

certain diseases such as malaria, which has spread more rapidly as a direct result of this increased global warming.

Other damage has also resulted from the warming of our atmosphere. Many regions have suffered damage from wildfires and major flooding events have increased both in frequency and intensity. The overall result is catastrophic. And as we stand, unless we take action to mitigate the effects of global changes to our atmosphere, things are likely to get much, much worse.

One of the many major concerns is that the increased global temperature is causing the polar ice caps to melt. This in turn is causing sea levels to rise. For example, it's estimated by NASA[2] that globally sea levels have risen by two inches in the last twenty years alone. If both polar ice caps and all the glaciers around the world are allowed to melt, it's estimated sea levels will rise by about 65 metres to 70 metres which would bring massive devastation to coastal cities right around the globe, resulting in the loss of vast swathes of land.

It is blatantly clear that the challenges caused by global warming are very serious indeed. It is therefore important that we try to look for ways to address this matter with a suitable degree of urgency. It's unlikely that one single solution will be found that will end this threat completely, but instead a number of techniques may be required to help slow down the catastrophic increase in the temperature of our climate, which hopefully will buy us sufficient time to find a way to halt global warming and eventually reverse it for the benefit for everyone alive today and for the benefit of the people who will come after us.

In this brief text, I explore some possible solutions which hopefully will help us to bring the worst effects of atmospheric warming under some level of control. This isn't likely to be the last word on this subject but hopefully it might help to reduce the catastrophe that we all currently face.

2. Rain Fall

The scale of the challenge posed by the widescale warming of our atmosphere is clear, but what can be done about it? Perhaps the most obvious answer is to stop pumping greenhouse gases into the atmosphere and find some way to remove all the pollutants that we've already put there. This might sound easy enough but implementing this solution would be far from straight forward.

For a start, we'd need to radically alter much of the way we live, particularly in the more industrially advanced parts of the world, where much of our economic success is dependent on large scale, energy intensive manufacturing processes and massive carbon generating transport links.

Also, there's no obvious way to remove all the pollutants from the atmosphere in one fell swoop. Each gas is chemically distinct and behaves differently with its own unique physical characteristics. Take for instance the case of carbon dioxide[3] (CO_2), which has become a major cause of global warming. The amount of CO_2 in the atmosphere has increased by more than 50% compared to pre-industrial years[1]. This gas stays in the atmosphere for a very long time – anything between 300 years and 1,000 years[4], or longer and it's estimated that 2,400 billion tons of CO_2 have been emitted by human activity since 1850[5]. This level of pollution has been produced mainly as a result of the burning of fossil fuels; predominantly coal and gas. Other causes, such as the manufacture of cement and the breakdown of methane have also contributed to these high levels. It is possible to filter CO_2 out of the atmosphere, but as is the case with the cleansing of all other greenhouse gases, every known process for doing this is highly energy intensive and therefore involves very high costs.

One mechanism which also contributes significantly to the effects of global warming is one that is generally overlooked, maybe because it's completely natural, and that is the process of rainfall. Water vapour in the atmosphere isn't a pollutant as such, indeed it's essential for the existence of the majority of life forms on Earth, but it's certainly the case that excessive amounts of water vapour in the atmosphere can intensify the impact of certain aspects of global warming, and as such, this may provide us with an opportunity to interrupt the serious, growing impact of climate change, until other, more effective long-term solutions can be identified.

Of the four widely recognised cloud formations, the cloud type Nimbostratus[6] is most closely associated with the production of rain. Clouds of this type vary widely both in terms of size and altitude, but it is possible to make some broad generalisations. Typically clouds tend to form at higher levels in warmer climates and at warmer times of the

3

year. The specific altitude can depend on several factors, including the type of cloud and the prevailing weather conditions, but most rain clouds form at least 300 metres above the ground and in many cases form at a height below 3,000 metres. The generation of cloud formations isn't always easy to predict, but a typical raincloud would form at a height somewhere around a height of 1,500 metres, approximately one mile above sea level.

Likewise, the size of raindrops varies significantly. A typical cloud droplet is small, with a radius in the region of about $1/100^{th}$ of a millimetre. A large aerosol particle would generally be about five times bigger and a small aerosol particle would typically be five times smaller than the typical droplet, or even less. Under the right environmental conditions, these droplets condense together within a cloud to form raindrops which condense out and descend towards the ground. The size of these raindrops also varies quite widely. A typical raindrop might have a radius of about 1mm[7], but the radius of other raindrops might be as small as 0.1mm and others might have a radius of 2mm or more.

Once a raindrop is released from a cloud, it begins to fall to the ground and initially it picks up speed as it accelerates downwards, pulled to Earth by the force of gravity. If it wasn't for the presence of air resistance, the velocity of the raindrop would continue to increase until the point when it hit the ground, as the potential energy associated with the falling water drop would all be converted to kinetic energy. However, as it speeds up, the raindrop experiences increasing air resistance which results from the viscosity of the air in the atmosphere. The raindrop stops accelerating once the force of the air resistance increases to such a point that it eventually equals the weight of the raindrop - the force with which gravity is pulling it downwards. Once this point is reached, the raindrop will have reached its maximum speed, and as such, it will have then reached its *terminal velocity*.

If we consider a typical raindrop with a radius of 1mm falling from a cloud floating somewhere at an altitude of 1,500m, the raindrop would reach the ground at a velocity of about 100.96 m/s. Such a raindrop would actually have a terminal velocity $V_{TERMINAL}$ = 118.96 m/s so it would have continued to accelerate all the way down, increasing its velocity, albeit at a slowing rate, until it eventually reached the ground. The amount of kinetic energy such a raindrop would have attained

4

when it reached the ground would only be about 35% of the potential energy it had lost in falling from the cloud. The remaining 65% of the energy would have been used to overcome air resistance and this energy predominantly ends up heating both the raindrop and the atmosphere. Exactly how this energy is split between the raindrop and the atmosphere is difficult to estimate precisely, but it's likely that both the raindrop and the air in the atmosphere experience some increase in temperature.

In appendix 1, the distance through which raindrops of different sizes must fall *in order to reach their terminal velocity* has been calculated. Also, the fraction of the loss of potential energy which is required to overcome air resistance has been deduced. This shows some interesting results. Within the limitations of all the assumptions that have been made to simplify these calculations, for example that any particular raindrop remains spherical and of fixed mass throughout its descent to the ground (something that we all know is not strictly true but hopefully will not seriously impact the results reached here) every falling raindrop requires the *same percentage* of its potential energy to *exactly achieve its terminal velocity* in air.

Every raindrop falling through air, irrespective of its size, will only have converted 14% of its potential energy to kinetic energy at the exact point where it reaches its terminal velocity.

What's more, having reached their terminal velocity, the raindrops won't convert any more of their potential energy to kinetic energy. All the potential energy that isn't converted to kinetic energy will instead be used to overcome air resistance, and will in effect be used to heat up both the raindrop and the air through which it falls. Of course, an increase in temperature may cause the raindrop to change its size (which in the case of water could be an increase or decrease in size depending on the exact temperature of the raindrop, particularly in the region of 4°c, due to the anomalous expansion of water) but generally speaking, such changes in size would be miniscule and wouldn't drastically alter the conclusions reached here.

The difference between large raindrops and small raindrops is that large raindrops have to fall a much greater distance in order to reach their terminal velocity. Whilst a tiny raindrop with a radius of only $1/10^{th}$ of a millimetre, only has to fall slightly over *half a metre* to reach its terminal velocity of 1.19 m/s (about 2.64 miles per hour) an average rain drop with a radius of one millimetre has to fall more than 5,215.4 metres to reach its terminal velocity of 118.96 m/s which is more than 266 miles per hour.

There would therefore be a possible advantage to be gained in respect of the heating of the atmosphere caused by falling raindrops, if we could find a way to make raindrops bigger, or ensure that clouds form at lower altitudes, so that less of their loss in potential energy gets converted directly into the heating of the atmosphere. In the case of clouds forming at lower altitudes, there'd also be the *potential* added advantage (no pun intended) of having less energy to convert into heating the atmosphere in the first place, in addition to reducing the proportion of this energy that directly goes into heating the climate.

Of course, in some respects, all this energy eventually ends up back in the atmosphere through one mechanism or another, either as the raindrop evaporates soon after hitting the ground, or once it cools and emits its heat energy, whether through radiation and the emission of photons or through convection or even perhaps conduction by passing energy to the molecules of air or other minerals and elements that might surround it, once it has reached the ground. *But it might be the case that there is a very real possibility of making a meaningful difference here*, because by intervening to mitigate the most intense buildup of localized increases in atmospheric temperature, it might just be possible to control the worst violent effects of the most devastatingly destructive storms. If we can interrupt a sudden onset of this heating effect, we might be able to take action to reduce injury, save lives and maybe reduce the damage to homes and other infrastructure upon which large numbers of people depend for their immediate welfare and ongoing wellbeing.

It isn't to be imagined that this will provide anything other than a partial stopgap solution, but at the very least, if we can begin to identify strategies for controlling the worst impacts of climate change, then this might help buy us enough time to reach a better, more robust, long-term solution.

P.J. Naughton

3. How Bad Can Rainfall Really Be?

In appendix 2 I've tried to calculate the worst-case scenario, aiming to estimate the *maximum* impact that energy released from falling rain could have on our climate. Clearly this is an overestimate, as it assumes every single unit of energy from falling raindrops goes directly into the heating of the atmosphere; but the intention of this calculation is to establish the highest possible contribution that falling rain could make towards global warming.

Of course, rainfall isn't spread evenly around the globe. Here in the U.K. we benefit from a rainfall which is quite a bit above the global average. Even here, year-on-year levels of rainfall vary quite widely, but generally we annually receive somewhere in the region of 1.4 metres of rain. Over the globe as a whole, the average level of rainfall is more like 1.0 metres per year. Seemingly, some hot desert regions have long suffered from serious, prolonged droughts. Some places on Earth have to wait months, and in some cases even several years for meagre amounts of precipitation to fall, and there is strong evidence to suggest many of these places are suffering worsening levels of extreme drought. Largely this has been brought about as a direct result of climate change largely caused by human activity, either in recent years in varying degrees by people currently living on Earth, or to some extent, by some of our more recent ancestors.

By establishing an upper limit on the possible heating effects of falling rain, we might be able to begin to formulate some type of control mechanism which might, in some way, enable us to put a limit on the worst and most impactful storms.

In appendix 2 it's estimated that in the extreme worst case, in the artificial circumstance *where all the energy from falling rain is absorbed by the atmosphere*, then the global average one metre annual rainfall, falling from an average cloud 1,500 metres above ground, could theoretically increase the temperature of air below the clouds over the course of a year, by about 8 Kelvin (which is exactly the same as an 8°c increase). However, *when we also consider the latent energy of vaporisation released by water vapour* condensing to liquid rain, exactly as it does in rain-bearing clouds, we find *the energy released in this way is about 154 times larger than the energy released by the loss of potential energy from rain falling from the average cloud.*

Clearly, the latent energy which is released when water vapour inside our clouds condenses to liquid rain, is extremely important in contributing towards the heating of our atmosphere. If we could find some way to control the release of this latent energy, this might provide us with some means by which we might hope to control the onset of storms.

4. The Greenhouse Effect

Undoubtedly, the so called "Greenhouse Effect" has a serious impact on the global temperature of our climate. Basically, every object with a temperature above absolute zero (a temperature of about -273.16°c) will emit thermal radiation over a wide range of wavelengths. The wavelength at which the *peak of energy emission* occurs depends on the temperature of the object, as predicted by Wein's law. The sun is very hot, it has a high temperature, so it emits the peak of its energy at a high frequency and therefore at a low wavelength. This radiation penetrates the Earth's atmosphere with relative ease and as a result, a lot of this energy reaches the surface of the Earth where it's largely absorbed.

However, in comparison to the sun's temperature, the surface of the Earth is relatively low. So, the peak of energy emitted by the Earth occurs at a much lower frequency. Unfortunately, a good deal of this radiation is absorbed by carbon dioxide and several other greenhouse gases in the atmosphere, and some of it is re-radiated back to the Earth's surface. In effect the carbon dioxide and other greenhouse gases act much like a blanket around the Earth, in much the same way that glass behaves in a greenhouse. As levels of carbon dioxide and other greenhouse gases are increased in our atmosphere, then the effect on the Earth becomes ever more catastrophic.

A calculation is shown in appendix 3 which serves to illustrate the effects of this form of global warming. Carbon dioxide and water vapour in the atmosphere both serve to absorb and re-emit the predominant infrared radiation which is emitted from the Earth's surface at its prevailing average ~13.9°c temperature, thus acting to curtail the radiation from the Earth that would otherwise keep the planet much cooler, in contrast to the visible radiation emitted from the sun, which largely cuts through the atmosphere to directly heat the Earth's surface without suffering so much in the way of absorption or scattering.

Clearly it would be advantageous if we could regulate the greenhouse effect in some way. Reflection of sunlight might be an attractive choice. Once sunlight is absorbed by the surface of our Earth, it is re-radiated at a much lower temperature, at a longer wavelength that is substantively blocked by the increasing levels of greenhouse gases. If we could reflect the sunlight instead, it would largely retain the high frequency and lower wavelength consistent with the values which it possessed when it was emitted by the sun. The retention of this high frequency would mean it would be less likely to be blocked by greenhouse gases on its way back out into space, for exactly the same reasons it wasn't blocked very much on its journey towards the surface of the Earth in the first place.

In respect of visible light, the reflectivity of mirrors can be very close to 100%. Similarly, the reflectivity of some polished metals can be very high. For example, the reflectivity of polished aluminium[8] can be as high as 90% The reflectivity of other materials can vary. Water[9] that is kept perfectly still, can have a reflectivity as high as 70% but water that is disturbed can have a reflectivity as low as 5% The amount of visible light absorbed by even very clean water is about 50% through a depth of 10 metres. This equates to about 0.005% absorption per millimetre of water. It could be the case that such values might afford an opportunity to make a meaningful intervention. It might prove useful to look closer at an example of a recent extreme weather event in order to gauge the true extent of the challenge we face.

5. Hurricane Helene

Looking back over recent centuries, on average, Florida[10] is affected by major tropical storms or hurricanes about once every three years. Many serious weather events have been recorded in that state over the last two hundred years or so. Since 1850, cyclones have led to about 10,000 deaths in the vicinity of the sunshine state and its neighbouring states, and these storms have caused damage thought to be in excess of 300 billion dollars or more. This situation has worsened in recent years, with significant hurricanes widely reported in 2022, 2023 and 2024.

Arguably, the worst ever hurricane to strike Florida occurred in September 2024. It was truly devastating. Storm Helene[11] began to form on 22nd September. On 25th September it was upgraded to a hurricane. This catastrophic weather event caused widespread destruction across Florida and the neighbouring states of Georgia and both North and South Carolina, with recorded *sustained* windspeeds in excess of 140 mph. Despite forecasts warning of the impending storm, the resulting impact caused over 230 deaths, knocked out power for millions of people and led to widespread damage, with estimated costs for repair of damage to be in the region of some $88 billion dollars. This was one of the most powerful storms to ever hit the United States and the loss it caused was truly catastrophic.

Typically, hurricanes can be hundreds of miles wide. They can deliver over a trillion watts of power[12], more than two hundred times the electrical generating capacity of the entire planet. Helene dumped more than 40 trillion gallons of rain over Florida and surrounding states. Most affected areas suffered between 6 and 12 inches of rain. As a result of this storm, Busick in North Carolina, suffered in excess of 30 inches of rainfall over a very short period. This excessive rainfall largely resulted from heating of seawater to record temperatures in the Gulf of Mexico. Control of the condensation of the water in the storm clouds, might have made it possible to curtail such an extreme deluge.

A calculation has been made in appendix 4 (Reversing Precipitation) to estimate what would be needed to reverse this level of precipitation inside rainclouds. It's clear that in practise, the amount of energy required *to reverse the precipitation* of such a vast amount of rain on the scale that was generated in hurricane Helene, will remain impractical for the foreseeable future. Basically, to totally reverse this amount of precipitation would require a rapid injection of energy over a matter of a few days, equivalent to about *360% of the total annual energy consumption of the USA* – clearly an unrealistic proposition.

It's often claimed that *prevention is better than cure*. It seems that in the case of hurricane level storm control this adage might be particularly true. In appendix 5 (Preventing Precipitation) an estimate has been made of the level of energy required to *avoid precipitation occurring* at such a rate, on such a massive scale. However, just to maintain this amount of water vapour at a level just one degree above the dewpoint would *still* require a massive amount of energy, amounting to 0.325% of the total annual energy consumption of the United States.

Over a 5-day period, this vast amount of energy could be reflected by the sun from an array of 100% reflectors stretching over an area of about 920 square miles. The minimum cost of this, assuming a minimal price of $1 per square metre ($m^2$) would be about $2 billion dollars. Whether this is a realistic cost would very much be open to debate. Whatever the true outlay required, it's beyond doubt this would be a major investment, but if it helped to prevent injury and save lives, and if it could reduce the scale of losses (an estimated $88 billion loss was caused by Helene alone) then it might well prove to be a worthwhile consideration. By way of comparison, the Trump wall cost about $21.6 billion dollars, which goes to show investments on this scale can actually be made if there is sufficient political impetus and popular support.

Deciding where to locate this type of solution would require careful consideration and would require buy-in from the community as a whole. The distance along the southern coast of the U.S.A. from the town of Mobile to Cape Coral is approximately 650 miles. A stretch of reflectors positioned along this coast about 1.5 miles wide would probably provide some useful protection against the buildup of the most frequent, extreme storms. It would very likely prove more highly advantageous if a transportable solution could be created within economic constraints, so protection could be reconfigured on demand to further mollify specific storm threats.

In any event, there's a strong case to be made for installing highly efficient reflectors on a wide scale, to transmit solar radiation backout into space. Use of reflection is important to ensure that light from the sun is transmitted at the same spectrum of wavelength with which it arrived, which would ensure the maximum amount of light managed to escape absorption by greenhouse pollutants and thus minimize the rate of warming of our shared global climate.

A similar case could be made for installing reflectors at both arctic poles. This would need to be done on a massive scale to have any hope of reducing the impact of global warming. If left unchecked, the melting of the polar icecaps will have a huge impact on sea levels across the globe. The engineering challenges involved would undoubtedly be significant, not only to install such protection but also to ensure the ongoing efficiency of the reflectors, making sure the mirrors remained reasonably clear of ice and snow. But challenges of this kind are not unsurmountable and the likely benefits could be colossal. The design of so-called 'cats-eye' reflectors that provide a clear indication of carriageways, even in very poor light conditions, continue to be successful after decades of use, particularly because they are effectively self-cleaning. These reflector units are designed to recess into their housing whenever vehicles runover them and this action provides a wiping action which cleans the reflecting glass prisms. Hopefully it would be possible to design a similar self-cleansing mechanism for arrays of large-scale solar reflectors to provide the much-needed protection against global warming.

6. Control Rain With Wind

By their very nature, it's never easy to predict the precise nature of major storm events. However, whenever major storm events are analysed in detail, the same sort of patterns emerge. It's always the case that some places are impacted more severely than others. In the case of Hurricane Helene, as mentioned earlier, it was the town of Busick in North Carolina that was particularly badly hit. Despite the heavy rain across the entire region, Busick suffered more than double the rainfall that similar towns in the path of the storm suffered. If we can understand why this happened, it may provide some clues as to possible solutions. It seems no coincidence that the town of Busick is very close to Mount Mitchell[13]. Standing tall at 6,684ft (2,037m), this is the highest mountain in North Carolina.

Mountains invariably have a major impact on rainfall right across the entire globe. Basically, mountains and large hills cause clouds that travel across them to rise higher in the sky. When clouds rise, their temperature tends to drop and they are less able to retain their moisture, thus prompting rainfall. It's the same story everywhere. In the UK, the prevailing winds tend to travel across the country from west to east. The Pennines run like a backbone through much of the northern regions. They act to push clouds higher which encourages them to burst. This helps to explain why the annual rainfall in the east of the country is on average lower than in the west.

The drop in temperature with altitude will be obvious to anyone who has climbed a mountain. It's nearly always colder at the summit than it was when you started off at the foot of the mountain. This happens because air pressure reduces as we move higher up, which in turn causes gas to expand. Gas needs energy to expand and this leads to a loss in temperature.

In appendix 6 the theoretical variation of temperature with height is estimated and comes out to be about 1°c per 100 metres of height. Measurements vary depending on particular weather conditions including air pressure and humidity... etc. but in many regions, actual temperature will drop by about 0.5°c for every 100 metres of altitude climbed from sea-level.

The Great Pyramid at Giza[14] is 146m high, so it might be about 0.7°c cooler at the top. The Burj Khalifa[15], the highest building in the world at the time of writing, stands an impressive 828m high. So, we might expect a temperature drop of about 4.1°c at the top of this amazing structure. In the case of Mount Mitchell at 2,037m we might expect a temperature drop somewhere in the region of 10.1°c

Maybe, if it had been possible to raise the height of storm Helene's clouds by about 2km whilst they were travelling over the Gulf of Mexico, they might have dropped much of their rainfall harmlessly into the sea and a great deal of the devastation it caused to places like Busick might have been significantly reduced.

But this begs the question, could the height of clouds be manipulated in some way?

The wind speeds in storm Helene were certainly very high, reported at a sustained value of 140 mph which is an extremely high value. In appendix 7 the possibility of deflecting these winds is investigated. However, given the energy needed to overcome air resistance, it's unlikely that the deflection of even these high-speed winds would prove of much use in helping to control the rainfall in any meaningful way.

7. Control Rainfall By Cooling

The moisture droplets in clouds tend to condense out and fall as raindrops when they're cooled. If we could artificially cool clouds in some way, we might be able to force them to disgorge any excessive rainfall in areas where this would likely cause least damage, such as over open seas. Ideally it would be useful if we could identify a gas that would be less dense than air, that would have a lower Specific Heat Capacity than air, that could be released to rise up to cloud level and because of the lower Specific Heat Capacity would have lost more temperature than air at a specific height and would therefore cool the clouds.

We'd also need to ensure the release of any such gas would not have any adverse environmental impact, either in terms of global warming or on impact to any forms of life. Unfortunately, it's not been possible to identify any such gas.

The density of air (please see table 1 below[20]) is actually quite low relative to the value for most gases (ρ_{air} = 1.293 kg/m^3). All the common gases with densities lower than air have higher values of Specific Heat Capacity at standard temperatures and pressures S.T.P. so unfortunately, it seems there is no obvious gas that could be released in large volumes, in an area of imminent risk from storm, in order to pre-empt the threat and initiate rainfall before clouds reached any heavily populated area.

For example, hydrogen has a much lower density than air but its Specific Heat Capacity is much higher so it wouldn't lose much of its temperature as it rose up through the atmosphere, gaining potential energy as it floated upwards. This means any released hydrogen would probably arrive at the cloud base with a higher temperature than the clouds, so it would serve to heat them up rather than cool them down.

In addition, hydrogen can react to further increase greenhouse gases – for example it can react with carbon deposits in the atmosphere to create methane, which, although it has a shorter lifespan than carbon dioxide, can be worse in terms of causing greenhouse warming and in any event, will eventually degrade back to carbon dioxide.

In the table below the typical, widely accepted values[20] for the densities and specific heat capacities of common gases are listed.

Different sources sometimes show slightly varying values, but these approximate values, or fairly similar measurements are quoted in the most widely recognised global sources.

Ref	Gas	Density (kg/m³)	SHC (J/kg/Kelvin)
1	Hydrogen	0.090	14,300
2	Helium	0.179	5,240
3	Methane	0.717	2,200
4	Ammonia	0.771	2,190
5	Water vapour	0.800	2,020
6	Acetylene	1.173	1,590
7	Carbon Monoxide	1.250	1,050
8	Nitrogen	1.250	1,040
9	Ethylene	1.260	1,500
10	Air	1.293	993
11	Nitric oxide	1.340	972
12	Oxygen	1.429	913

Table 1 – The Density and SHC of common gases at S.T.P.

One alternative way of controlling rainfall is through a process called seeding[38]. Basically, if appropriate chemicals are dispersed into clouds, then in theory, rainfall can be induced from them. Several different versions of this technique have been attempted since the 1940's. Various chemical agents have been deployed, including silver iodide, potassium iodide, dry ice (solid carbon dioxide) and liquid propane. There are different opinions amongst scientists about the success of this approach. Also, there are some environmental concerns about the chemicals used, although in truth the quantities of chemicals for these purposes are very small indeed.

One chemical which has been used recently and shows promise is sodium chloride (table salt – available in huge quantities in oceans around the world). Common salt is hygroscopic – it attracts water molecules. If a bowl of salt is left exposed to the air, it'll become lumpy over time as it becomes moist, attracting water vapour from the air. For this reason, finely powdered salt has shown considerable success as a cloud seeding agent. It has the additional benefit of being readily available in the sea and as a natural component of seawater, there are perhaps less environmental concerns about it's wider scale use. That said, there are possible arguments in favour of decreasing the levels of salt in our seas, as this might lead to benefits in terms of reducing the amounts of water vapour that makes its way into our atmosphere.

8. The Possible Benefits of Desalination

Desalination involves the removal of salt from seawater and salt water lagoons. This seems likely to provide one of the most important opportunities for the control of major storms. Water has a relatively high Specific Heat Capacity SHC. Most significantly, the value for the Specific Heat Capacity of *fresh water, is actually higher* than the value for sea water by about 7.4%

$$SHC_{Fresh\ Water} = 4,190 \text{ J/kg/}^\circ c$$
$$SHC_{Sea\ Water} = 3,900 \text{ J/kg/}^\circ c$$

This could provide a possible mechanism for potentially reducing the critical high surface temperatures of the oceans.

In appendix 8 a calculation is shown for the possible impact of desalination of the Gulf of Mexico. Whilst the total desalination of such a large ocean would be a massive undertaking, *these results show that an achievable, ongoing, partial desalination operation could have a very significant result in reducing the intensity of major hurricanes.*

Reducing the salinity of the Gulf of Mexico by just 5% could reduce its surface temperature by more than 1°c. This would be an enormous task and it might not sound like it would achieve a significant reduction in temperature, but this target could be achieved over time and it would undoubtedly have a major impact on the suppression of the enormous ferocity of major tropical storms in the region. It could *reduce* the loss of life, significantly *reduce* the threat of physical injury and would limit the widescale damage to property and infrastructure which often results from the most intensive tropical storm events of the kind which have become ever more frequent in recent years and are likely to become ever more destructive if climate warming is not carefully managed.

This major improvement could be achieved using energy supplied directly from the sun. And if managed judiciously, it could provide a highly prized by-product – table salt, which is widely used in food production and as such has a very real commercial value.

One important question remains regarding this specific proposal. How much land would be required to reduce the salt levels in the Gulf of Mexico within a reasonable time period, say 20 years, relying exclusively on heat from the sun to desalinate sea water through evaporation?

An approximate estimate of the land required for these purposes is presented in appendix 9. Broadly speaking, an area of land at least 750 miles long and 750 miles wide would need to be designated to this project to reduce the salt levels in the Gulf of Mexico by 5% and bring about a 1°c reduction in the surface temperature of its waters. This is a massive area of land, but desert or arid scrub land could easily be used for these purposes.

Large-scale desalination operations are already ongoing in the state of Florida[19]. In the South Florida District alone, about 40 desalination plants currently produce about 292 million U.S. gallons (about 1.1×10^9 litres) of drinking water each day, mainly using a process of reverse osmosis. Deep well injection is used to deposit the attendant residue into the Boulder zone; a cavernous limestone formation some 3,000 feet below the surface.

The processing required to desalinate 5% of the Gulf of Mexico (5% is about 1.2×10^{17} litres) over a twenty-year period would require a substantial increase in the current processing capacity of desalination. We'd need to desalinate about 1.64×10^{13} litres of seawater per day – an increase in scale about 15,000 times bigger than current volumes. This is a massive increase, but given that the main aim would be to reduce salt levels from the ocean rather than to supply potable water to local residents, it would be quite acceptable to rely on evaporation by radiation from the sun, as any fluctuations in the rate of processing wouldn't have any impact on the supply of fresh sweet water direct to consumers.

Of course, a project on this scale would require substantial investment. Infrastructure would be required to move the Gulf waters to the sites chosen for processing and to properly process the substantial residues of salt. No doubt this would prove costly, but the benefit of such an initiative would be truly enormous. It would immediately start to play a part in reducing the intensity of storms and would undoubtedly continue to save thousands of lives over many generations into the distant future.

9. Removal of Greenhouse Gases

The removal of greenhouse gases from the atmosphere would clearly have a significant impact on global warming if it could be achieved on a sufficiently large scale. This is not easy to achieve, mainly because many of the proposed solutions are highly energy intensive, but some innovative proposals are showing very real potential.

One recent proposal, which is showing considerable promise, has been made by Sheffield University[22]. Researchers there have demonstrated that the scattering of crushed rock over the surface of farmland can capture and retain significant amounts of carbon dioxide. CO_2 in the atmosphere is absorbed to a slight extent by rainwater. After the rain falls to the ground, it evaporates and unless captured in some way, any carbon dioxide gas it contained is largely released back into the atmosphere, although in certain circumstances, small amounts are absorbed into the land. By covering agricultural land with small amounts of suitably crushed quarried stone, the volumes of carbon dioxide which are retained from the falling rain can be very much enhanced.

It might prove to be the case that other methods could be developed which could destroy some greenhouse gases. Unfortunately, many of the gases involved are extremely stable in terms of their chemical structure and don't readily lend themselves to easily achieved methods of destruction. The carbon dioxide molecule for example is particularly stable. Many molecules can be split up into their associated constituent parts if they are subjected to sufficiently high temperatures, but in the case of carbon dioxide, temperatures in excess of 700°c are required, which for all practical purposes, is not easy to achieve on an economic scale.

However, some other greenhouse gases might prove more susceptible to certain methods of dissociation. According to the U.K. Government, in a report[23] produced by the Department for Environment, Food and Rural Affairs in 2022, it's claimed that one of the most significant greenhouse gases produced by agricultural activities in the U.K. is nitrous oxide N_2O.

Greenhouse gas emissions in this report are displayed in units of $MtCO_2e$ This unit is widely used around the world. It stands for *million tonnes carbon dioxide equivalent*. The reason this unit is used, is to take into account the actual impact of each individual greenhouse gas, rather than just display the volume with which they exist. So, for example, although methane lasts in the atmosphere for a much shorter time than carbon dioxide, whilst it is present, it has a much greater capacity to warm the environment than an equivalent volume of carbon dioxide. Whilst carbon dioxide has a Global Warming Potential (GWP) of 1, this is the standard reference benchmark, the GWP of methane is GWP = 25.

In this DEFRA report, it's claimed that agricultural activity in 2020 accounted for 44.8 $MtCO_2e$ of greenhouse gases which is 16% lower than the 53.6 $MtCO_2e$ emissions of 1990. However, this 2020 rate still accounts for about 11% of total UK emissions. The greatest amount of greenhouse warming caused by UK agriculture in 2020 was generated by methane at 24.8 $MtCO_2e$ (down 15% from 29.0 $MtCO_2e$ in 1990) In 2020 agriculture was responsible for the generation of 48% of methane in the U.K.

Perhaps surprisingly, the second most impactful greenhouse gas produced by agriculture in 2020 is reported to be nitrous oxide. About 14.5 $MtCO_2e$ of nitrous oxide were produced by UK agriculture in 2020 which means this sector was responsible for 69% of the N_2O produced across the nation in that year, down 20% from 18.1 $MtCO_2e$ that was generated by agricultural activities in the U.K. in 1990. This particular greenhouse gas was largely produced in the agriculture sector following the breakdown of nitrogen-based fertilisers by micro-organisms in the soil.

U.K. agriculture was only responsible for generating 1.7% of the nation's carbon dioxide in 2020 with a volume of 5.5 $MtCO_2e$. This was down some 15% from 6.5 $MtCO_2e$ in 1990.

Clearly, a significant improvement had been made in decreasing the volumes of all the significant greenhouse gases generated by UK agriculture between 1990 and 2020 but hopefully new techniques will be developed which will allow further improvements to be made.

Nitrous Oxide N_2O

Of the most significant greenhouse gases generated by agricultural activities in the U.K. arguably the gas that could be most easily broken down into its constituent parts is likely to be nitrous oxide. Having a warming factor some 300 times greater than carbon dioxide, this gas makes a significant contribution to global warming.

Nitrous oxide is known to undergo photodissociation, caused by ultraviolet light from the sun. This occurs particularly at a wavelength of 203 nanometres[25][26] which is equivalent to a photon energy level of 6.108 eV

If we take a look at the energy levels required to cause ionization in each of the elements, we find that both thallium with an ionization energy of 6.108eV and calcium at 6.113eV both have first ionization energies on, or close to the specific energy specifically required by photons to break down nitrous oxide molecules (see table 1 below).

Element	Protons	Ion	Eion /eV	Eion/Joules
Plutonium	94	1	6.026	9.655E-19
Uranium	92	1	6.080	9.741E-19
Erbium	68	1	6.100	9.773E-19
Thallium	81	1	6.108	9.786E-19
Calcium	20	1	6.113	9.794E-19
Gadolonium	64	1	6.140	9.837E-19
Thulium	69	1	6.180	9.901E-19
Berkelium	97	1	6.198	9.930E-19
Yttrium	39	1	6.217	9.961E-19
Ytterbium	70	1	6.254	1.002E-18

Table 2 – First Ionization Energies Around 6.108 eV

Ionization involves the liberation of electrons from atoms. This can occur when electrons absorb a photon with the exact same energy they already possess. Any electrons that fell back into the atoms would release this same energy as a photon. If nitrous oxide were to be exposed to either of these elements whilst they were subject to radiation from the sun, it's possible that it might be broken down by the energy of the photons released. Thallium is highly toxic, but in contrast calcium[24] is the most abundant metal in the human body. It's also the fifth most abundant element in the Earth's crust, being widely available in several forms such as calcium carbonate $CaCO_3$ probably better known as limestone.

It might prove to be the case that the addition of crushed limestone added to nitrogen fertilisers might help to reduce the amount of nitrous oxide produced by agricultural establishments around the globe, in what would be a slight variation on the method proposed by researchers at Sheffield University, where the methods responsible for capturing carbon dioxide by the scattering of crushed rock have been identified.

Hopefully, if this process is proven to work in the case of nitrous oxide, then perhaps similar techniques could be developed to reduce the presence of other greenhouse gases.

10. Regulating Seawater Temperature

The temperature of seawater varies with depth[29][30]. The exact nature of this variation depends on amongst other things, the location of the particular part of the sea in question, the climatic conditions, the seasons, recent weather patterns and volume and chemical content of major flows along rivers and channels both in and out of the waters. But, whilst particular details may vary, a general pattern is observed almost everywhere around the globe.

At a basic level, most text books identify three layers of deep sea. In the graph below, a typical example of what might be observed in the tropics is shown.

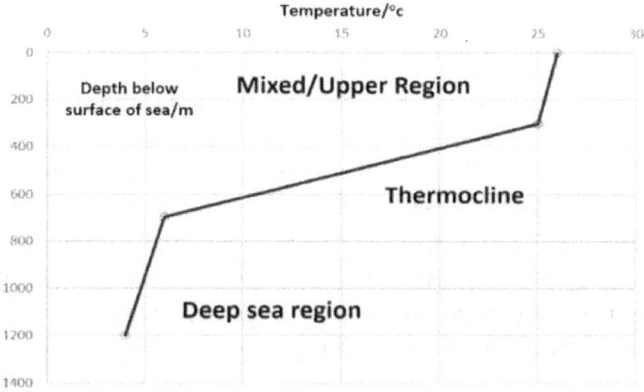

Graph 1 – Temperature of a Tropical sea

Stop The Storms

At the surface the temperature can be as high as 27°c in warm regions, or maybe even higher. This appears to be the critical temperature at which point serious storms are generated. Obviously in colder regions, the surface temperature would generally be much lower but the same basic pattern seems to exist in most cases. Whatever the surface temperature, it doesn't seem to vary more than a few degrees centigrade in the *upper* layer (sometimes referred to as the *mixed region*) down to a depth of maybe 300 metres or so. This is largely because sunlight can penetrate the seawater to quite a depth and swirling currents in the upper-level help maintain a fairly constant temperature.

At a depth of about 300 metres or so, the middle *Thermocline* region begins. In this region, the water temperature falls rapidly with increasing depth, falling by as much as 1°c for every further 20 metres travelled downwards. The Thermocline stretches down to about 700 metres where the *Deep-sea* region begins. The temperature in the lowest depths varies only very slowly as we travel further down. Starting at about 6°c, it eventually drops to about 4°c or maybe slightly below to 3.8°c.

Water has what is referred to as an *anomalous expansion*. It's at its most dense at 3.8°c and will get *less dense* once cooled below this temperature. This is very unusual. For most materials, their *density continues to increase* as they are further cooled. This explains why solid icebergs float in the sea and why ice cubes float in drinks at cocktail parties. More importantly, it is widely thought to be the reason why water is so essential to the evolution of life. If water did not behave in this way, ice would not form on the top of ponds and fish and other marine lifeforms might be more susceptible to freezing, whereas, as things stand, they can remain relatively frost free at the bottom of lakes, seas and deep ponds in the densest water at a relatively safe 3.8°c thus escaping being trapped in solid ice.

This raises an important question, *could cold water at the bottom of seas be used to regulate their surface temperatures in some way, and thus prevent the generation of dangerous storms?*

This prospect of using *conduction* to remove heat away from the surface of the sea is explored in some detail in appendix 10. Unfortunately, because water is such a poor conductor, and given the depths and relatively small temperature differences involved between the various layers of the seas, there doesn't appear to be any strong likelihood that conduction could be useful in any significant way.

In appendix 11 the possibility of pumping cold water from the lower regions of the oceans to cool the surface layer is analysed. Whilst this might provide some limited scope for controlling the excessive overheating of the surface of the seas, it's not a particularly attractive solution due mainly to the very high costs involved and the reliance on the availability of sufficiently very deep waters that would be needed.

11. Breaking Clouds

Perhaps the best way to control extreme storms would be to partially break up storm clouds before they ever had the chance to reach land. In appendix 12 a simple solution is proposed to achieve this. If wet strings/ropes could be suspended through storm clouds down to the sea, it might be possible to force clouds to *lose their electrical charge* thus causing them to drop the vast bulk of their massive content of rain prematurely, over the oceans.

As implausible as this process might sound, it was demonstrated to be viable to some degree many years ago, when **Benjamin Franklin** way back in the eighteen-century carried out an experiment to prove that lightening was associated with electrical charge. *Potentially, this could prove to be a very cost-effective solution.* With an investment of perhaps only a few hundred thousand dollars, the use of drones and the creation of a suitably trained coastguard team, it might be possible to avert much of the massive rainfall which causes so much flooding and wreaks so much havoc which leads to vast amounts of costly damage to so many communities throughout Florida and neighbouring states and to everyone else in all the other similar locations that are at risk from major storms located all around the globe.

Trialling this solution would not be expensive; the risks are only very modest and the potential benefits are truly enormous. Hopefully this solution and solutions like it, will minimize the risk that increasingly serious storms pose to so many communities.

This isn't meant to be an excuse to carry on pumping vast quantities of greenhouse gases into the atmosphere, far from it, but hopefully it will help to minimize the risk of injury to thousands of people in vulnerable area until better solutions can be found.

12. Rising Sea Levels

The rate at which sea levels are rising is a major concern. The increase in the level of seawater is a result of the melting of polar ice caps caused by climate change. If left unchecked, this will lead to major flooding in major coastal regions around the entire globe. Between 1993 and 2023, over a period of some 30 years, sea levels around the globe rose by about 101 millimetres. This increase equates to about 3.36mm per year. This might sound like a very small amount, but because 71% of the Earth is covered by oceans, the volume of water involved in this rise is truly enormous.

A calculation is performed in appendix 14 to estimate the amount of energy that would be required to convert *this annual increase in seawater* to its component gases, by means of electrolysis. It turns out that the energy required to convert this $1.22x10^{15}$ kg of water to gas by electrolysis would be 1.61×10^{22} Joules.

The amount of energy required to convert this amount of water to vapour through heating, via a temperature increase of 75°c from 25°c to 100°c given a Specific Heat Capacity of sea water to be SHC = 3,900 J/kg/K and then to convert all that liquid water at 100°c to gas at 100°c given a Specific Latent Heat of Vaporization L = 226 J/kg would only be about $3.57x10^{20}$ Joules i.e. about 2.22% of the energy required to change the water to its component gases by electrolysis. However, water vapour is a greenhouse gas and would only add to the issues of global warming. Electrolysis has the advantage of providing the opportunity to capture the separated amounts of hydrogen and oxygen.

In appendix 15, a calculation is performed to estimate the average useful power generated by wind turbines. With an average useful power output of about 2.44 Mega-Watts from a large unit, the number of installations needed to generate the energy required to prevent rising sea levels by the electrolysis of the additional water would be about 209 million wind turbines. These would cost about £10.5 trillion GBP pounds (about $13.3 trillion US dollars). This is an enormous investment. It represents about 47.4% of the entire *annual* 2023 GDP of the United States or about 12.2% of the 2023 *annual* GDP of the entire world.

This might well sound totally unachievable, but if spread over the average 25-year lifetime of wind turbines, it could be achieved for 0.49% of the annual world GDP at an annual global investment of £0.42 trillion GBP pounds or $0.54 trillion US dollars. Again, this is still a huge financial commitment, but if we compare it to the annual spend on defence, which globally amounts to some £1.89 trillion ($2.4 trillion US dollars) we see it's only about 20% of the global defence expenditure.

If every country in the world agreed to divert one fifth of their defence budget into tackling climate change, it would be possible to build sufficient wind turbines to significantly slow down rising sea levels. Even a huge investment of this kind probably wouldn't totally stop the rise in the level of the sea, as it assumes that the rate at which the seas are rising will remain constant, whereas in reality it seems likely that, if left unchecked, this rate is actually increasing. But it would certainly have a significant impact on limiting the rise in sea levels and would help to minimize the problems caused by widescale flooding that would otherwise result.

Of course, with every proposal that involves massive environmental engineering on such a large scale, there is always likely to be unintended consequences. If we electrolysed all the rising seawater into its component gases, we'd generate a vast amount of hydrogen and oxygen.

Let's suppose that we released the oxygen into the atmosphere and kept the hydrogen back to be used for fuel purposes. Of course, burning hydrogen would convert it back into water again, so care would be needed to ensure all this water doesn't end up going straight back into the seas again, to add back to the problem of rising sea levels but for now let's assume this issue can be managed in some way.

Annually the *increase* in the number of moles of water in each square metre of sea is about 187.04 moles. Water is made of H_2O so there are two atoms of hydrogen for every atom of oxygen.

Oxygen has an atomic mass of 16 grams per mole whilst hydrogen has an atomic mass
of 1.00797 grams per mole. So, each year the *increase* in the amount of oxygen in every square metre of sea surface is about 2.987 kg.

$$Pressure\ P = mg/A$$

This means if we released the oxygen into the atmosphere from the electrolysis of the increased sea water every year, the annual increase in atmospheric pressure would be

$$\Delta P = 29.357 \ N/m^2$$

The standard atmospheric pressure varies slightly depending on the seasons and weather patterns ..etc. but the standard atmospheric pressure is 101,325 N/m^2

If we assume the same increase in pressure was made every year, after 10 years the total pressure increase over this period would be 293.57 N/m^2 This amount of increase in atmospheric pressure would probably only have a slight impact on our environment. At this pressure, instead of boiling at 100°c water would boil[39] at 100.08°c

After 25 years of adding the same amount of oxygen in this way, the increase in atmospheric pressure would be about 0.72% or an additional 733.925 N/m^2 taking the average atmospheric pressure to 102,059 N/m^2

This atmospheric pressure would increase the boiling point of water from 100°c to 100.2°c This is perhaps, in general, not a significant change that would have any real impact on the average person on a day-to-day basis. An increase of this kind might help to prevent storms to some minor extent, as the increased pressure would mean less water would evaporate into the atmosphere.

There would likely be additional consequences, although in truth most of them would only have a very subtle impact. For example, a small pressure increase like this would slightly increase the absorption of oxygen in tissue. This would likely prove beneficial to humans and most animal life in the short term as long as the pressure increase was only very small. There would be no risk of oxygen toxicity at this level, although people sensitive to pressure changes, such as those with sinus issues, middle ear problems, or respiratory concerns, might feel *slight discomfort*, similar to the effect caused by a small altitude change. This sensation would be comparable to the feeling people often experience when descending a few hundred feet in altitude.

A 1% increase in air pressure would subtly affect wind patterns and the behaviour of storms. Since atmospheric pressure drives weather, areas with frequent low-pressure systems might see slightly less intense storms.

Increased atmospheric pressure would cause a very small *compression effect* on the ocean's surface, leading to a slight apparent drop in sea levels which would only be a few millimetres or less; certainly not sufficient to compensate for the rise in sea levels caused by melting polar icecaps.

This small increase in atmospheric pressure would slightly increase the density of air by about 1%. This would marginally affect sound propagation, thermal insulation, and aerodynamic properties. Aeroplanes and vehicles might experience *slightly* higher drag and increased lift due to the denser air, which could impact fuel efficiency and flight dynamics.

Infrastructure designed to withstand atmospheric pressure would remain unaffected, as a change of this size is within normal operating tolerances.

A pressure increase of 1% would have negligible effects on most plants and animals, since their respiratory and metabolic systems are adapted to small variations in pressure (e.g. daily weather changes or altitude shifts). Gas exchange processes in the lungs and environment (like CO_2 uptake by plants) would see a slight increase in efficiency, but this would not have noticeable biological impacts.

A small 1% increase in air pressure is a small and largely tolerable change for humans, ecosystems, and technological systems in general. Its effects would be subtle, with minor benefits like slightly improved oxygen availability and denser air for aerodynamics. Weather systems and sea levels might experience very slight changes, but nothing catastrophic or disruptive.

However, this kind of solution would not be a permanent long-term solution. It would certainly help to control sea levels for 25 years or so, but a 10% increase in atmospheric pressure over a 250-year period would lead to a much different outcome. The impact on humans and all other forms of life caused by a 10% increase in atmospheric pressure would be truly devastating, so we could not hope to keep adding to the atmospheric pressure for many generations to come. Instead, better long-term ways of managing the gases that might result from the wholesale electrolysis of sea water would need to be found.

Cooling Caused By Wind Turbines

Of course, if we were to remove the vast amount of energy from the atmosphere on the scale that would be needed to power electrolysis, sufficient enough to prevent any rise in sea levels, then we'd inevitably reduce the temperature of the climate.

An estimate of the reduction in the temperature of the climate is provided in appendix 16. Here, we see that **a theoretical reduction in the temperature of our climate of -3.06°c, double the entire increase caused by hundreds of years of global warming, could theoretically be achieved in a period of just one year.**

Obviously other factors would play a part to reduce this decrease quite considerably. For a start, the sea acts as a vast heat sink and as such, massive amounts of heat would move from the sea into the air in order to try to compensate for the change in the atmospheric temperature. The land would act in much the same way. But there's no getting away from the fact, significant amounts of energy could be removed from the entire system in this way, and if controlled appropriately, the overall result could be extremely beneficial in helping to bring climate change under a level of control that has never before been achieved. And this has to be a good thing, and in the absence of a better solution, it might prove to be the only chance we really have of avoiding total global chaos.

Hydrogen Fuel

If all the hydrogen gas produced from the total electrolysis of rising seawater were captured in some way, it could more than meet the world's current annual energy requirements.

A calculation of the energy which could be produced by this process, is provided in appendix 17. This shows that the hydrogen released from rising seawater would supply more than 18.1 times of the world's total annual energy requirement.

Of course, when hydrogen is burned in oxygen then it reverts back to water. Care would need to be taken to ensure any water produced in this way, wouldn't contribute further to global sea levels. The fact that only 1/18th (about 6%) of the hydrogen produced in this way would be needed to meet the world's energy needs means that, even in the worst case, if 100% of the water produced by burning hydrogen to meet our total energy requirements ended up back in the sea, then at least 94.5% of the increase in the sea level would still be prevented.

28

There then remains the question of what could be done with the remaining hydrogen gas? Some of it could possibly be put to good use to produce even greater amounts of clean energy which could be used to cleanse greenhouse gases from the atmosphere, particularly the high levels of carbon dioxide.

Care would be needed to ensure that massive amounts of any excess hydrogen gas was not released into the atmosphere as it can contribute to greenhouse warming. Hydrogen is the lightest element, so it rises quickly in the atmosphere due to its low molecular weight. It diffuses and disperses rapidly, mixing with the surrounding air. Hydrogen reacts indirectly with the atmosphere. Free hydrogen reacts with hydroxyl radicals (OH), which are crucial for breaking down greenhouse gases like methane. This can thus contribute to some extent to global warming. The Global Warming Potential (GWP) of methane over 20 years is estimated to be about 85 (CO_2 has GWP = 1) but over the long term, it is much less significant than CO_2 in terms of global warming, due to its short atmospheric lifetime. Methane in the atmosphere oxidizes into CO_2 and water vapor fairly quickly, over a period of about 12 years, meaning its warming effect is concentrated in the short term in comparison with CO_2 which can survive in the atmosphere for hundreds of years. However, the presence of hydrogen can extend the life of methane by reducing the presence of hydroxyl radicals which are responsible for breaking it down.

The atmospheric lifetime of hydrogen is approximately 1–2 years. It does not react directly with oxygen at ambient temperatures, making it relatively stable in the atmosphere. A small fraction of atmospheric hydrogen can reach the upper atmosphere where Earth's gravity is weaker. Hydrogen atoms can achieve escape velocity and can therefore be lost to space over time, contributing to the Earth's gradual loss of hydrogen.

Whether or not electrolysis is ever used to control sea levels, the management of hydrogen emissions will become increasingly important if we are to avoid unintended environmental consequences, as its use as a source of green energy becomes increasingly popular.

13. Taming The Winds

It's all well and good attempting to reduce excessive rainfall, but unless gale force winds can also be controlled, then we can never really say storms have ever been completely tamed. For, in the case of a large number of storm events, it's often the *hurricane force wind* which causes at least as much damage as heavy rainfall and the flooding that so often follows.

As mentioned previously, rain clouds are comprised essentially of droplets of moisture. When they cool, these tiny droplets coalesce to form raindrops, which inevitably at some point, fall to the ground in a shower of rain. The radius of these droplets is typically about 10 microns, less than the radius of a human hair. Despite this very small size, these tiny droplets still have some mass, albeit a very small one. So, we might ask ourselves, *why is it that these tiny droplets of water don't fall down to the ground, if they have mass and must therefore be pulled down by the force of gravity?*

The answer to this question is an important one, as it reveals some important aspects of the mechanics of our weather system; the existence of which we all completely rely on, as it is essential to maintain our very ongoing existence.

The answer is of course that the tiny droplets in clouds are indeed influenced by the Earth's gravity and as such, they are pulled down towards the ground, but due to their extremely small size, this process is a very slow one, particularly as another force acts on them to help maintain their position high up above the surface of the ground.

In appendix 13 the terminal velocity of a typical water droplet is calculated. With an average radius of just 10 microns, and assuming the density of water to be 998kg/m³, such a droplet would only have a mass of 4.18×10^{-12} kg. Given that air has a coefficient of viscosity of η = 1.51×10^{-5} Nsm⁻² then the terminal, maximum velocity of the falling droplet would only be very low, coming in at about $V_{TERMINAL}$ = 0.0144 m/s assuming the drop remains spherical throughout its descent.

This means, in order to fall from a height of 1,500 metres (a typical cloud might form at this height, about a mile from the ground or often much higher) the droplet would take about 28.9 hours – more than a complete day to complete its fall, even if no other force acted on it! However, other forces do indeed act on such droplets. One force which is always present is Archimedes upthrust which as Archimedes described, *equals the exact weight of the fluid or gas displaced.*

However, in this case the gas displaced is air, which only has a density of about 1.293 kg/m^3 at S.T.P. so compared to water, with a density of 998 kg/m^3 the Archimedes upthrust would only be about 0.13% of the weight of the droplet, so would not have any real significant impact here.

One force though, which does have a big impact on the behaviour of water droplets, is the updraft caused by radiation from the sun heating the ground, which in turn warms the air in contact with it, thus reducing its density and causing warm air currents to drift upwards. This updraft is very significant indeed. In appendix 13 the speed of this updraft is estimated for a column of air standing above a point on the ground that is receiving the maximum radiation from the sun.

It turns out that when the maximum radiation is arriving from the sun, the column of air above it could theoretically be moving upwards in its entirety at a velocity of;-

$$V_{UPDRAFT} = 0.0138 \text{ m/s}$$

Adjusting the terminal velocity by this amount would leave a *net* downward velocity of about;

$$V_{NET} = 0.0006 \text{ m/s}$$

The difference in the estimated terminal velocity of the average droplet falling unhindered to Earth and the velocity of an entire column of air forced up by heat from the maximum radiation from the sun is only about 4.3%

Taking this adjusted relative velocity into account, this means it would take about 29.36 days for the average droplet to fall just one mile from a typical rain cloud. *This perhaps serves to illustrate how finely balanced our weather system, which we all completely depend on, really is.*

Of course, these calculations are very simplistic. It's not likely that any column of air above any point on the ground would ever be expected to move up at any uniform speed. Far from it. We wouldn't expect any tall column of gas to be heated uniformly when receiving most of its energy from the base. The likelihood is that whilst pockets of warmed air would definitely spiral upwards, clusters of cooler air would swirl downwards to fill any gaps. And in any case, the maximum radiation from the sun arrives only very fleetingly, if at all, on any particular day at any chosen point on Earth.

Despite the obvious limitations of the simple calculations shown here, they do perhaps serve to illustrate the fine balance of the forces involved; forces which we rely on, the very forces involved in providing for all our needs, which are essential in keeping all of us and all other life forms around the world, all adequately nourished; a process that, whilst it no doubt must have varied from time to time in both scale and intensity over the millions of years of evolution, must have continued at least to some degree, largely uninterrupted since life on our planet first evolved.

Notwithstanding the limitations on the precision of any of the estimates made here, it's clear that the updrafts from warm air currents play a key role in helping to maintain the stability of cloud formations and the weather system which results.

For the most part, it's clear that in most regions of the world, a status of orderly calm tends to persist for most of the time. However, this does not always prove to be the case. At times when the heat rising from the Earth's surface becomes excessive, the resulting updrafts can spiral out of balance. This is an important factor in the generation of significant changes in air pressure, which in turn can lead to the generation of a major storm vortex. If swirling wind patterns continue to build unrelentingly, the possibility of the generation of a massive catastrophic storm becomes a very real one.

Understanding the mechanics which lay behind the generation of major storm events, even on a simple level, may enable us to identify some means of intervening to mitigate the biggest threats and thus reduce the worst impact of the ensuing consequences.

The way in which the wind speed varies with the distance from the centre of a cyclone is well documented[40][41][42]. Typically, the velocity of wind in a major storm vortex will reach a maximum value some distance from the eye of the storm. The wind speed at the very centre (the eye) will generally be very low, almost zero, but as we move away from the centre, the wind velocity increases almost linearly until it reaches some maximum value, after which point the velocity decreases quite rapidly.

A simple schematic representation of this variation in velocity is shown below.

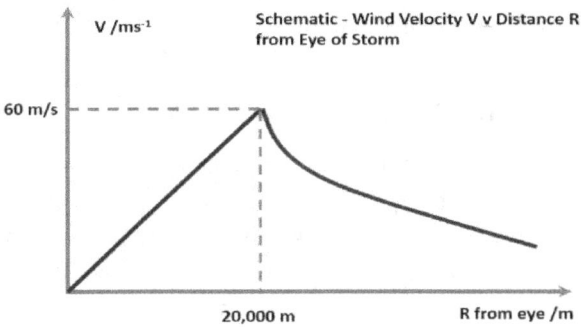

Graph 2 – Wind Velocity v Distance from centre of storm

Exact values vary considerably depending on the exact nature, size and age of a storm but the values shown, with a maximum wind velocity of V = 60m/s at a distance 20 km from the central eye of a storm might be typical values for a major cyclone.

In appendix 18, the approximate distribution of energy in a storm vortex is estimated. From this basic calculation it appears that as much as 34% of the total kinetic energy of a storm will be present within 10% of the distance where the maximum wind velocity occurs. If this is in anyway correct, it means it might be possible to target the areas where the maximum energy of a storm resides. This is a very approximate estimate - it relies on a number of very simple assumptions. Others will be able to improve on this very basic calculation, but at least it provides some hope that it might be possible to identify the location of a large percentage of the energy within any typical storm system.

It might well prove advantageous if the highest velocity winds in a cyclone could be diverted in some way. It might be possible to achieve this to some extent using magnetic fields to deflect the high volume of electrically charged water droplets that exist in strong wind currents.

In appendix 19 the characteristics of an experimental device that might provide the required magnetic field are presented. This is a relatively small-scale, low-cost device but if it proved effective, it might be possible to design devices that would prove effective over a much larger range and thus provide some means of controlling the flow of storm force winds.

14. Our Distance From The Sun

A crucial factor, which to some extent plays a part in determining the surface temperature of any particular planet, is its distance from the sun. Planet Earth is no exception. All the planets in the solar system maintain their orbit around the sun because they have sufficient lateral motion. They are all pulled towards the sun by gravity but they do not fall into the sun because they have sufficient speed to maintain a constant orbit. In general, the orbits the planets describe are elliptical as established by Johannes Kepler. Some of the planets in our solar system, like Venus for example, have a near circular orbit. Others less so. The Earth also has a fairly circular orbit. At its furthest point from the sun, the so-called aphelion which occurs about 4th July each year, the distance between the Earth and the sun is approximately 152.1 million kilometres (94.5 million miles), whilst at the nearest point, the perihelion which occurs around January 3rd each year, the distance between the Earth and the sun is approximately 147.1 million kilometres (91.4 million miles). So, there is only a variation of about 3.1 million miles or about 3.3% in the distance between the sun and the Earth as it completes each orbit.

If any planet gained sufficient velocity, it might be able to escape from its orbit around the sun. Alternatively, if any planet suddenly lost significant amounts of kinetic energy, it would be pulled into an orbit closer to the sun. As this planet moved closer to the sun, it would lose Potential Energy. This energy would mostly be converted into Kinetic Energy. Eventually, it might gain sufficient velocity to establish a new stable orbit closer to the sun. If any planet lost sufficient kinetic energy, it could be pulled into the sun where it would be consumed in the sun's cauldron of fire.

This applies to the Earth just as much as it applies to any other planet in our solar system. If the Earth were to suffer a collision with any other major space object, it could lose momentum and end up falling into an orbit closer to the sun. Of course, as any planet moves closer to the sun, the intensity of solar radiation arriving on its surface increases accordingly and inevitably its surface temperature increases.

Imagine for a moment if the Earth suffered a massive collision and lost all its orbital velocity. It would then undergo freefall, picking up speed as it plunged into the sun. This final journey would take a little over 60 days to complete. It would take just over a month to complete half this journey, by which time its average surface temperature would have increased from the current 287 Kelvin (about 14°c) to about 406 Kelvin, which is about 133°c – hotter than boiling water (see appendix 20). It's unlikely that any form of life would be able to survive at this temperature. Subject to this level of heat, surface water would rapidly evaporate into what little remained of the atmosphere. Seas, rivers and lakes would quickly boil dry, all plant life would be killed and as the Earth continued its journey, plunging inexorably ever further towards the sun, the temperature would continue to escalate rapidly.

The size of any celestial body capable of causing any such disaster, would have to be enormous. The Earth hurtles around the sun at a very high average velocity,

$$V_{EARTH} = 29,785 m/s$$

which is about 30 times faster than a speeding bullet.

Earth also has a relatively large mass...

$$M_{EARTH} = 5.97 \times 10^{24} \text{ kg}$$

This produces a momentum (mass x velocity) of 1.78×10^{29} kg m/s

Any space object undergoing freefall towards the sun, would accelerate as it moved closer to its target destination. If it had begun its fall from the further reaches of the solar system, it would have reached a velocity of about $V = 42,119$ m/s by the time it reached the distance of 1 A.U. from the sun – the Astronomical Unit is the average distance between the sun and the Earth.

To cancel out the Earth's momentum entirely, such a celestial body would have to make a head-on-collision and have a mass of about 71%

the mass of Earth. Few planets would be big enough. Mars, for example, only has a mass of 6.417×10^{23} kg (about 10.7% of the mass of the Earth). On the other hand, Venus has a mass of 4.867×10^{24} kg (about 81.5% of Earth) so it would certainly be big enough to bring the Earth to a halt, but it's located nearer to the sun than Earth, so it's unlikely it would ever collide with us.

Even if any such body did hurtle towards the sun in this way, it's very unlikely it would ever collide with us, even in the unlikely event that it did happen to be in the same plane as the Earth's orbit around the sun. The Earth has to travel 940×10^{12} m (about 584 million miles) to complete one orbit around the sun, but it only has a diameter of 12.742×10^6 m (about 7,918 miles) so the odds of a collision with a celestial object falling towards the sun would be less than 0.0014% (about 1 in 74,000) even if such a body were to cross the Earth's orbital path.

If we were ever so incredibly unlucky to suffer such a major cataclysm, all might still not be entirely lost. For a start, the angle between the trajectory of the Earth and the freefalling planet would probably be close to 90 degrees, depending on the exact position of the Earth around its elliptical orbit. As such, this would not be a head-on collision. Hopefully, unless we were extremely unlucky, any such collision would most likely be more of a glancing blow. Undoubtedly, any such event would cause massive, widespread devastation, but there might be some hope that life on Earth could still prevail, despite the massive loss of life that would inevitably result.

Meteors

Over its lifetime, we know that the Earth has suffered a number of major meteor strikes, all of which are subject to wide reaching research and are actively discussed and debated [43][44][45][46]. Perhaps the largest meteor strike on Earth was caused by the Vredefort meteor which struck about 2.02 billion years ago. It's thought this meteor would have had a diameter of about 12 to 15 miles and a mass of about $10^{16} - 10^{17}$ kg and that it struck with a velocity of about 20,000m/s. This would no doubt have had a major impact on the Earth, but despite its colossal size and speed, it still wouldn't have had much impact on the orbit of the Earth, given that the momentum of the Earth (mass x velocity) would have been about 89 million times larger.

Other large-scale meteors also had a devastating impact on life on Earth. The Chicxulub meteor, probably the second largest meteor to strike Earth, occurred about 66 million years ago. It is thought to have had a mass of $10^{12} - 10^{13}$ kg and it's estimated it landed with a velocity somewhere in the region of 20,000 m/s. There is no doubt this must have been a major event, yielding energy in the region of about 300 Zetta Joules (300 x 10^{21} Joules) and as such, it would have caused an explosion much larger than any nuclear bomb, in fact about 1.5 million times larger than the largest man-made explosion, the so-called Tsar Bomba, which in 1961 yielded energy of 50 megatons (equivalent to 50 million tons of TNT).

The Chicxulub meteor is widely thought to have led to a mass extinction and was the cause of the extinction of the last of the dinosaurs, along with probably more than half of other lifeforms on our planet, but even so, it's unlikely this would have had much impact on the Earth's orbit since the Earth's momentum would have been 900 billion times larger.

We are aware that there are some extremely large asteroids in outer space[47]. Ceres, for example, located in the asteroid belt between Mars and Jupiter, has a mass of 9.1x10^{20} kg. If it suddenly fell towards the sun and having achieved a free fall velocity approaching 42,119 m/s at the point of collision with the Earth, it could at worst alter the momentum of the Earth by about 0.02% There's no doubt this would be a colossal event, leading to widespread global devastation, but nonetheless, the resulting impact on the Earth's orbit would, in all probably, only be fairly minor.

So, despite the seeming vulnerability of our planet and the fragility with which life somehow continues to persist, it's clear it would take an extremely massive event, larger than anything that has occurred in its entire 4 billion-plus year lifetime, to threaten the entire existence of life on our planet. However, we should perhaps also be aware of the impact, seemingly much more minor events could have on the chances of our ongoing survival.

The Moon

Arguably, one of the greatest risks we potentially face which could result from a change in the behaviour of any celestial body, might be posed by our nearest neighbour, our moon. The moon is relatively large compared to the moons of other planets, in fact any distant observer who viewed our solar system from far out in space might be forgiven for concluding that our planet and the moon are part of a double-planet system, given the comparative size of our moon.

No one really knows how the moon came into existence - maybe a passing asteroid was captured by the Earth's gravity. Other theories exist, but perhaps the most likely explanation is provided by the 'Big Splash theory'[47]. Sometime in its early life, the Earth could have been struck a glancing blow by a large object, something roughly the size of Mars. Molten material ejected by both the Earth and the colliding object, would have condensed and eventually evolved to form the moon that we see today.

The moon orbits the Earth in 27.32 days (the sidereal orbit) in a slightly elliptical orbit but due to the movement of the Earth around the sun, it takes 29.53 days to complete its synodic cycle. In truth, it's slightly inaccurate to say the moon orbits the Earth because the moon is so large, with a mass about 1.23% the mass of Earth, this means the Earth and the moon orbit around a common point – *the barycentre*, which is inside the Earth, but about 2,902 miles from its centre (about 1,056 miles below the surface).

The moon travels with an average velocity of about 1,027 m/s around the Earth, which is approximately the speed of a bullet. This means that the average momentum of the moon (mass x velocity) is very much smaller than that of the Earth - by a factor of about 2,350. This potentially makes the moon slightly more vulnerable to total loss of Kinetic Energy that might result from collision with another large celestial body.

Any object that originates from distant space, that is freefalling to the sun, would reach 42,119 m/s by the time it reached either the Earth or the moon. Any such asteroid with sufficient mass, anything around 1.79×10^{21} kg, could in theory totally cancel out the momentum of the moon depending on the direction it was travelling. An asteroid with this mass would be about 1.97 times heavier than the estimated mass of the Ceres asteroid. There's no doubt this would have to be a very big asteroid, bigger than anything we already know about, but this calculation does perhaps in part, go some way to illustrate the higher levels of vulnerability that exist for the smaller space objects that are present throughout the Universe at large.

It has to be said that the chances of any such occurrence are extremely remote indeed, mainly because the moon is only small; as such it presents a small profile to passing asteroids and its low mass means its gravity is only very small, so it's unlikely to pull space objects towards itself. However, we might ask ourselves, if the moon did suffer such a calamity, if it were struck by a massive asteroid that cancelled out its orbital momentum around the Earth, what might be the impact on ourselves? Would the outcome be totally cataclysmic?

The resulting trajectory of the moon would depend on the exact circumstances of the collision that occurred, the size of the colliding object, its momentum, the exact angle at which the collision occurred etc, but it's likely that having lost most or all of its orbital Kinetic Energy, the moon would fall to the surface of the Earth, pulled down by gravity in much the same way the planets would fall into the sun if they lost their orbital momentum. A calculation is provided in appendix 21 which seeks to estimate the worst-case impact this scenario might have on the Earth's orbit around the sun and the impact it might have on the temperature of our climate.

In the very worst case, if the moon did suffer a collision with another celestial body which brought it to a complete stop and as a result, it subsequently fell to Earth and in the very unlikely event it collided head-on with us, travelling in exactly the opposite direction in which the Earth travels around the sun, it could potentially cause the Earth's orbital velocity to reduce by about 485 m/s. This in turn could cause the Earth to move to a stable orbit approximately 4.76×10^9 metres nearer the sun (about 2.96 million miles) which would result in the temperature on the surface of the Earth increasing by about 4.68°c

The loss in Potential Energy of the Earth in such an event would be about 1.762×10^{32} Joules which amounts to some 278 billion times the total annual energy consumption of the entire world.

Obviously, a collision on this scale would be truly catastrophic. Without doubt, it would cause widescale devastation across the entire world. This sudden increase in global temperature would certainly add to the destruction. But this is *the worst case*. Of course, it's not in any way guaranteed that the moon would crash into the Earth and if it did, it's unlikely to impede the motion of the Earth to such an extent.

Stop The Storms

In the opposite *extreme case*, if the moon were to strike Earth 'from behind' such a collision might serve to push the Earth into an orbit further away from the sun, which would then potentially *reduce* the temperature on Earth by about 4.68°c instead.

It's difficult to know what actions might be taken to guard again any such threat in order to best protect ourselves against the occurrence of such a disaster or make preparations to perform the most appropriate mitigation actions should such a disaster occur, but at the very least, performing simple paper exercises of this kind and estimating the possible impact of such major events, may, in some way, help us to respond in the best possible way in the highly unlikely event that any such disaster were to occur.

As bad as a disaster of this kind would inevitably be, it might help to offset the immediate danger that imminent global warming threatens, if the Earth's orbit could be modified to slightly increase the distance between the Earth and the sun. Performing a manoeuvre of this kind in a controlled way, would not be easy to achieve but it might be something to consider as a potential longer-term strategy in order to modify the most extreme consequences of global warming.

15. Risks And Follies

The initiative aimed at tackling global warming is filled with risk. Afterall, we've never done anything like this before and we really have to get it right first time. We don't have the luxury that we might otherwise have if we had the time to get this wrong. The consequences of any major mistakes could be disastrous. As such, it's imperative that we remain fully alive to the possibility of any unintended consequences. We can't experiment on a truly global scale - *there is no planet B*. No doubt mistakes will be made, but we can't afford to get this catastrophically wrong, otherwise there might be no one left on Earth to learn from the mistakes that have been made.

The actions taken so far in the struggle to tackle climate change, appear to lack the appropriate level of urgency. At some point this must change. This is likely to come about in short order as the effects of global warming will no doubt increase dramatically in the immediate years ahead. We have already seen a dramatic increase in the frequency and intensity of major storm events and the devastation that such disasters have caused. This trend is likely to increase. However, any headlong rush to tackle the environmental issues we face, is likely to bring with it the increased risk of catastrophic mistakes.

Even within some of the modest steps we've so far managed to take in order to tackle this issue, there appear to be some possible errors. Take for example the desire to capture green energy with wind turbines. There's no doubt this is a commendable approach that is already helping the fight against global warming. But as laudable as this benefit is, it is far less effective than it could be. Why? Well, in the rush to implement positive change, the powers-that-be have made a decision to transport increasing amounts of energy over great distances using *high voltage overhead powerlines* suspended high above the ground. These powerlines are generally not insulated in any way. They rely for a large part on the air around them to provide electrical insulation so they don't arc to the ground beneath them.

One might think this shouldn't present any kind of problem. And it wouldn't do, if it wasn't for the fact these high voltage powerlines also lack any meaningful form of *thermal* insulation. Quite the contrary. In fact, *they rely on the air around them to keep them cool*, to stop them from overheating and permanently sagging or even melting. Lower operating temperatures also help to maintain the lower electrical resistance of power cables. Even so, these lines operate at fairly elevated temperatures – anything between 30°c and 90°c and in emergencies, when power transmission is at its highest, they will in some cases reach temperatures as high as 150°c for short periods.

The temperatures at which high voltage overhead powerlines operate are some of the worst for generating infrared radiation with the precise wavelengths that contribute most significantly to global warming.

Wein's Displacement Law describes the relationship between the temperature T of a perfect radiator and the wavelength λ_{max} at which it emits maximum radiation;-

$$\lambda_{max} \times T = K_{wein}$$

Where T is the temperature of the radiator measured in Kelvin and K_{wein} is Wein's constant which is 2.878×10^{-3} meters-Kelvin

Methane for example, absorbs radiation most strongly at a wavelength of 7.66 μm. This radiation is produced most intensely by a perfect radiator at 375.72 Kelvin which is exactly the same as 102.56°c This means that an object with a temperature just above the S.T.P. boiling point of water produces the infrared radiation which is most susceptible to absorption by methane.

One of the absorption wavelengths of nitrous oxide, another well-known greenhouse gas, is 7.8 μm. Infrared radiation with this wavelength is produced most intensely by a perfect radiator with a temperature of 368.97 Kelvin which is equivalent to 95.81°c

Gas		λ/m	$T = K_{wein}/\lambda$	$T/°c$
Ozone	O_3	9.60E-06	299.8	26.6
Sulphur Dioxide	SO_2	8.70E-06	330.8	57.6
Nitrous Oxide	N_2O	7.80E-06	369.0	95.8
Methane	CH_4	7.66E-06	375.7	102.6
Nitrogen Dioxide	NO_2	7.50E-06	383.7	110.6

Table 3 – Radiation Absorbed Greenhouse Gases

Table 3 shows the *wavelengths* of light which are strongly absorbed by *some* common greenhouse gases and the *temperature* at which perfect radiators emit these peak wavelengths (the wavelength at which they emit the highest amount of their energy). Ozone O_3 for example absorbs radiation very strongly at a wavelength of 9.6 x 10^{-6} metres (i.e. 9.6 μm). The temperature of a perfect radiator which emits its peak radiation at this wavelength (9.6 microns) is 299.8 Kelvin which is exactly the same as 26.6°c.

Sulphur dioxide strongly absorbs radiation emitted as a peak by a radiator at a temperature of 57.6 centigrade. This is the temperature at which many high voltage cables operate. Sulphur dioxide is a byproduct of burning fossil fuels. It's also produced by many industrial manufacturing processes and is emitted in large quantities by active volcanoes.

Although Wein's law describes the behaviour of perfect radiators, in general it also predicts the behaviour of real radiators to a very high degree of accuracy.

Overhead high voltage transmission lines are being installed on a massive scale in order to transport increased energy produced by wind-turbines as part of the initiative to achieve zero carbon emissions, but it is clearly *self-defeating* when one of the by-products of this initiative is to generate infrared radiation which is most susceptible to being trapped by two of the *worst* greenhouse gases.

The hottest place officially recorded on Earth[48] was 56.7°c at a place called Furnace Creek, Death Valley (USA) on 10th July 1913. This is an extreme temperature, but as global warming intensifies the occurrence of temperatures in excess of 50°c are becoming ever more frequent. However, as bad as these temperatures are, they are well below the highest temperatures at which many overground high voltage powerlines operate, at which point these electrical cables generate the most damaging thermal radiation – the very radiation that is most susceptible to greenhouse gas absorption.

In appendix 22 a calculation is made to estimate the power lost through thermal radiation from *overhead* powerlines in the U.K. It would appear that power lost from these lines would be sufficient to meet the total energy needs of about 1.5 million U.K. homes.

Rather than continuing to invest in *outdated* and *environmentally harmful infrastructure*, we should prioritize sustainable alternatives such as underground powerlines which are installed with proper thermal insulation to prevent the emission of harmful infrared radiation. These systems, while potentially more expensive upfront, provide greater efficiency, reduced energy loss, and significantly lower environmental impact.

By addressing these issues proactively, we can ensure that renewable energy projects, like wind and solar farms, achieve their full potential without inadvertently contributing to the very problem they aim to solve.

In appendix 23 a brief comparison has been made between overhead cables made of copper and the equivalent cables with the *same electrical resistance* made from aluminium. It should be noted, we are comparing cables with the same electrical resistance here, *not* cables of the same radius.

Given the lower resistivity of copper, which has a resistivity about 64% the resistivity of aluminium, the same resistance can be achieved with a copper cable that has only 80% of the radius of an aluminium cable of the same length. However, given the much higher density of copper (3.3 times higher than aluminium) the copper cable comes out to have more than double the mass of the aluminium cable, which is a disadvantage in terms of the mechanical support needs and the cost of the pylons/transmission line towers.

The thinner copper cable would run at a higher temperature than an aluminium cable with the same resistance, due to its reduced surface area. A copper cable would run at 79°c if it carried the same power and had the same initial resistance (at say 0°c) compared to an aluminium cable with an operational temperature of 60°c. This would mean the overall power loss from copper cables would be 0.54% whilst it would only be 0.50% from aluminium.

However, when we consider the wavelength of peak thermal emission in this case, a detail of considerable interest is revealed. The peak thermal emission from aluminium at 60°c would be at a wavelength of 8.64 μm whilst from copper running at 79°c it would only be 8.17 μm. Sulphur dioxide is an important greenhouse gas which is widely produced from the burning of fossil fuels and as a byproduct from various industrial processes, from organic decay and often in large quantities from erupting volcanoes. It strongly absorbs infrared radiation at a wavelength of 8.7 μm (emitted most strongly by a perfect radiator at 57.64°c) so despite the slightly higher losses from the thinner copper cable and the higher operating temperature, it would be a better choice in this case to limit the greenhouse energy absorbed by sulphur dioxide.

This kind of example serves to illustrate that the design of power transmission lines is not a simple matter. All relevant factors must be taken into account in the design of power grids, if we are ever going to be successful in bringing global warming under control.

It is vitally important that we achieve *appropriate optimum* efficiencies when we build new energy grids. We should not be cutting corners.

It's interesting to estimate the effect the energy loss from Overhead Powerlines has on our atmosphere. The energy loss is about 5% but given the amount of power transmitted by Overhead Powerlines, it's blatantly obvious this loss of energy is likely to increase the temperature of our atmosphere. An estimate of this increase is provided in appendix 24.

It's estimated that energy losses from Overhead Powerlines alone could contribute an increase in the temperature of our global atmosphere by more than 0.5°c over the next fifty years. Clearly this is a very significant increase given our current perilous position in respect of increasing levels of global warming and the catastrophic consequences that are certain to result unless we bring this situation under control.

We should not invest in *overground* high voltage powerlines that contribute so significantly to greenhouse warming.

16. Saving Grace

There is no doubt about it that even small increases in the temperature of our climate definitely have a very severe impact on our wellbeing. We are increasingly seeing the results of global warming in every aspect of our daily lives.

However, we are extremely fortunate that we live in a world that is, to some extent, self-regulating to such an extent that it works to limit the most extreme increases in temperature.

Diagram 1 – Planet Earth

Let us assume the Earth is a sphere with radius r. This is very near true.

The Earth receives radiation from the sun. The solar energy[52] incident on unit area normal to the sun's rays at the Earth's mean distance per unit time is;

$$P/A_{IN} = 1,400 \ W/m^2$$

The area *normal* to the sun's rays is the area of a *circle*.

Therefore …

$$P_{IN} = 1.4 \times 10^3 \times \pi r^2 \qquad \text{where r is the radius of the Earth.}$$

But any body with a temperature above absolute zero also emits radiation. For a perfect blackbody radiator Stefan-Boltzmann's law describes the rate of emission;

$$P/A = \sigma T^4$$

where A is the total surface area, T is the temperature in Kelvin and σ is Stefan's constant[52].

$$\sigma = 5.66969 \times 10^{-8} \ Wm^{-2}K^{-4}$$

The surface area of a sphere is …

$$A = 4\pi r^2$$

So, if we assume the Earth is a perfectly spherical blackbody radiator we can say …

$$P_{OUT} = \sigma \times T^4 \times 4\pi r^2$$

Therefore, for the Earth …

$$P_{OUT}/P_{IN} = 4 \times \sigma \times T^4/1.4 \times 10^3$$

If we put in different values for the temperature of the Earth T we get different values for P_{OUT}/P_{IN}

T/Kelvin	T/°c	P_{OUT}/P_{IN}
273	0	0.90
280	7	**1.00**
300	27	1.31

Table 4 – Earth's Net Radiation

From table 4 above we can see that the Earth becomes a net radiator once its temperature exceeds 7°c

Of course, this doesn't mean that global warming is not a major issue. The blanket of greenhouse gases that surround our planet traps energy on a considerable scale and means that our global temperature will exceed this otherwise very comfortable temperature. But it does perhaps illustrate that nature is on our side.

Conclusions

In summary, the main conclusions reached in this work are;-

➤ A large-scale array of reflectors designed specifically to reflect sunlight, could help to moderate the onset of the most violent storms in areas known to be at high risk of such events.

➤ Reflecting sunlight back into space could help to reduce the warming of our climate by minimizing the radiation absorbed by greenhouse gas pollutants in our atmosphere over a sustained period.

➤ The rate of latent energy released by the condensation of water vapour in major storm events can be very substantial - many times more than the current maximum rate of power generation on our planet.

➤ Partial desalination of the oceans which are particular hotspots for the generation of major storms, could help to reduce the devastation caused by the most intense tropical cyclones.

➤ Capture and photodissociation technologies could help to significantly control the presence of greenhouse gases in the atmosphere.

➢ Control of major rainfall events could be achieved by removing electrical charge from storm clouds, causing them to release their load of water directly into the sea before they reach land. Suspending appropriate conducting ropes through storm clouds hung all the way down to the sea, could achieve the required electrical discharges and help to minimize the severe flooding that might otherwise result from a major storm.

➢ By diverting 20% of the world's annual spend on defence and investing this finance into building wind turbines instead, *we'd be able to meet the entire energy needs of the world within two years* and bring to an end our current reliance on fossil fuels.

➢ We would need to continue to invest 20% of the annual global defence spend on wind turbines indefinitely, continuing to replace them after their 25-year lifespan, in order to generate sufficient energy to combat the rise in sea levels through the use of electrolysis.

➢ It might be possible to partially disrupt the wind flow in cyclones by constructing portal devices that would generate suitable magnetic fields to deflect electrically charged water droplets.

➢ Modifying the orbit of the Earth to slightly increase the distance to the sun might help to offset some of the worst effects of global warming, but in practise would be extremely difficult to achieve.

➢ We need to replace the outdated overhead high voltage powerlines that generate the worst form of infrared radiation that continue to drive greenhouse warming.

➢ The best way to avoid the worsening impact of global warming is to stop burning fossil fuels across the entire globe at the earliest possible opportunity.

For the most part, the state of the universe is largely the result of the forces which created it and the natural processes which have gone on to shape it. To some extent, the world we inhabit is different. The state of the Earth has also been altered to some degree or other by every single life form that has been privileged enough to call this planet their home.

What we see around us in our immediate surroundings today, has been affected by every animal and plant that has ever lived here. Looking around us, what we see is the sum result of every single action performed by every living entity both past and present; including all the creatures, many and varied as they are, whether they have flown these skies, swum the many rivers, lakes and seas or whether they have made their homes in the jungles or great grass plains, lived in deserts or burrowed underground or cleared land, planted crops and built vast towns and cities.

No species has shaped this planet we live on more than us humans have done. More than ever, more than any other generation that has gone before us, the immediate actions we take now will have a profound impact on the life chances of every single future generation as well as every single lifeform that comes after us. We have the opportunity to improve the lives of all our children and our children's children but time is not on our side.

We must be brave enough to take the big actions needed to ensure the ongoing viability of our planet for future generations to inhabit safely.

Stop The Storms

Appendices

The physical parameters used in these calculations have mostly been taken from some of the most widely recognised sources[20][28] although in some cases, in the interests of simplicity, the values used here have been rounded in keeping with the broad high-level assumptions that have been made. The intention is to present high-level estimates of various requirements in order to provide the orders of magnitudes involved rather than rigidly striving to derive altogether strict precise values.

Appendix 1 – Terminal Velocity of Raindrop

When a raindrop forms, it falls to the ground under the force of gravity. As it falls, the speed of the raindrop increases, as its potential energy PE is converted to kinetic energy KE. If it wasn't for air resistance, every raindrop would continue to accelerate as it fell from the sky. However, air resistance plays an important part in limiting the speed each raindrop can reach. The force of air resistance increases as a falling raindrop gets faster. This serves to gradually reduce the *acceleration* of the raindrop. Eventually, the raindrop reaches such a speed that the force of air resistance pushing up on it, exactly equals the force of gravity pulling it downwards. At this point, the raindrop can't accelerate anymore and at this point it's said to have reached its terminal velocity which we'll designate as $V_{TERMINAL}$.

Fortunately, it's reasonably easy to estimate the terminal velocity of raindrops if we assume they have a spherical shape. Raindrops are sometimes depicted as teardrops, but in reality, this isn't strictly true. Surface tension tends to keep raindrops spherical, but as they fall their bottom end is pushed flat by air resistance and they tend to wobble so their shape distorts accordingly.

Diagram A1.1 – The 'Classical' depiction of a Teardrop

In the interests of simplicity, these distortions in shape will be ignored here and it'll be assumed that raindrops remain spherical throughout their entire descent down to the ground.

We know that the force of gravity F_g on a raindrop is responsible for its weight.

We can say;-

$F_g = mg$ ... A1.1

where m is the mass of the raindrop and g is the acceleration due to gravity which close to the Earth's surface is about g = 9.81 m/s^2

According to Stoke's law, the force of air resistance F_{AIR} on a spherical object moving at velocity V is given by;

$F_{AIR} = 6\pi \times V \times r \times \eta_{AIR}$ ... A1.2

where r is the radius of the sphere and η_{AIR} is the coefficient of viscosity of the air through which it's travelling. The value of η_{AIR} = 1.8325 x 10^{-5} Nsm^{-2} at a temperature of 300 Kelvin.

When the force of gravity equals the force caused by the air resistance on a falling spherical raindrop, it'll stop accelerating. Therefore, from equations A1.1 and A1.2 we can say...

$V_{TERMINAL} = mg/6\pi r\eta$ ... A1.3

We can use a similar technique to calculate *the distance* through which a raindrop must fall before it reaches its terminal velocity.

The resulting force F_R which causes a falling raindrop to accelerate is given by the difference in the force of gravity pulling it downwards and the force of air resistance. (I'm ignoring the Archimedes upthrust here, caused by the displacement of air as this is trivial in comparison.)

$F_R = ma = F_g - F_{AIR}$ ... A1.4

where a is the acceleration of the drop of water, which can also be represented as dV/dt

Therefore we can say;-

$$m \times dv/dt = mg - 6\pi vr\eta \quad ... A1.5$$

If we say for any given raindrop, we have a constant weight A = mg
Also, for the sake of simplicity say B = 6πrη for our raindrop.

So we can say;-

$$m \times dv/dt = A - Bv \quad ... A1.6$$

dt can be replaced by dx/V as we're interested in distance fallen. Plugging this into equation A1.6 and rearranging gives...

$$\int dx = m \int \frac{v \, dv}{(A - Bv)} \quad ... A1.7$$

Integrating both sides...

$$x = - (m/B^2) \times [A\log(A - Bv) + Bv]_0^v \quad ... A1.8$$

where x is the distance fallen for a raindrop to reach velocity v

We know the terminal velocity from equation A1.3 which we can re-write as...

$$V_{TERMINAL} = A/B \quad ... A1.9$$

There is a slight problem here because if we use this value, in theory the terminal velocity is never reached. But let's assume we work with a velocity V_0 which we'll assume is 99% of the terminal velocity and therefore close enough for all practical purposes.

$V_0 = 0.99 \times A/B$ ... A1.10

Substituting this into equation A1.8 gives the distance a raindrop needs to fall to reach 99% of its terminal velocity...

$x = (m/B^2) \times [A\log_e(100) - 0.99 \times B \times V_{TERMINAL}]$ ... A1.11

We can use a similar method to calculate the work (energy) E_{AIR} which is done by the raindrop as it cuts through the air...

$$E_{AIR} = \int F_{AIR}\, dx \quad \text{... A1.12}$$

Substituting for F_{AIR} from equation A1.2 and dx from equation A1.7 we can say;

$$E_{AIR} = \int mBv^2/(A - Bv)\, dv \qquad \text{... A1.13}$$

Integrating we can say ...

$$E_{AIR} = -m/2B^2 \times [2A^2 \log(A - Bv) + Bv(2A + Bv)]\Big|_0^V \quad \text{... A1.14}$$

Again, using the maximum velocity $V_0 = 0.99V_{TERMINAL} = 0.99 \times A/B$ in order to overcome the limitation on the terminal velocity never being reached we can say...

$$E_{AIR} = (A^2/2B^2) \times [2\log_e(100) - 2.9601] \qquad \text{... A1.15}$$

We can also calculate this energy in another way. The amount of energy expended by the raindrop as it cuts through the air to reach its terminal velocity is the difference between the Kinetic Energy it achieves when it reaches its terminal velocity
i.e. $KE_{TERMINAL} = \frac{1}{2} \times m \times V_{TERMINAL}^2$ and the Potential Energy ΔPE released when the raindrop drops through distance x to reach this terminal velocity.

As expected, the value of energy needed to cut through the air E_{AIR} given by equation A1.15 *matches exactly* with the value given by the difference in the loss of Potential of the raindrop and the Kinetic Energy it achieves at its terminal velocity...

$$\Delta E = mgx - KE_{TERMINAL} == E_{AIR} \quad ... A1.16$$

It turns out that every raindrop, *irrespective of its size*, uses exactly the same percentage of its loss of Potential Energy in order to cut through the air to reach its terminal velocity. This fraction is perhaps surprisingly very high at 86%

i.e.
$$E_{AIR}/\Delta PE = 0.86 \quad ... A1.17$$

This means that only 14% of the change in Potential Energy of the raindrop goes into increasing its Kinetic Energy as it falls through distance x to reach its terminal velocity. *The much greater amount 86% of the change in Potential Energy goes into heating the raindrop and heating the air that it passes through.* How this heat energy is split between the air in the atmosphere and the water droplet is difficult to say. Of course, once the falling raindrop reaches its terminal velocity, then 100% of all the subsequent change in its Potential Energy is converted into heat energy as the velocity of the raindrop cannot be increased beyond its terminal velocity and therefore its Kinetic Energy remains constant.

The table below shows the calculated distances x through which raindrops of different radius r (measured in metres) must fall in order to achieve their terminal velocity $V_{TERMINAL}$ (measured in metres/sec)

r	Vol = 4/3πTr^3	Mass	A=mg	B=6πTrη	x	PE = mgx	VTerm =A/B	Vo=0.99 xVTerm	KE=1/2m Vo^2	Eair = (PE - KE)	Eair/PE
1.0E-04	4.19E-12	4.19E-09	4.11E-08	3.45E-08	0.52	2.14E-08	1.19	1.18	2.91E-09	1.85E-08	86.4%
2.0E-04	3.35E-11	3.35E-08	3.29E-07	6.91E-08	8.34	2.74E-06	4.76	4.71	3.72E-07	2.37E-06	86.4%
3.0E-04	1.13E-10	1.13E-07	1.11E-06	1.04E-07	42.2	4.69E-05	10.71	10.60	6.35E-06	4.05E-05	86.4%
4.0E-04	2.68E-10	2.68E-07	2.63E-06	1.38E-07	133.5	3.51E-04	19.03	18.84	4.76E-05	3.04E-04	86.4%
5.0E-04	5.24E-10	5.24E-07	5.14E-06	1.73E-07	326.0	1.67E-03	29.74	29.44	2.27E-04	1.45E-03	86.4%
6.0E-04	9.05E-10	9.05E-07	8.88E-06	2.07E-07	675.9	6.00E-03	42.83	42.40	8.13E-04	5.19E-03	86.4%
7.0E-04	1.44E-09	1.44E-06	1.41E-05	2.42E-07	1,252.2	1.76E-02	58.29	57.71	2.39E-03	1.53E-02	86.4%
8.0E-04	2.14E-09	2.14E-06	2.10E-05	2.76E-07	2,136.2	4.49E-02	76.14	75.38	6.09E-03	3.89E-02	86.4%
9.0E-04	3.05E-09	3.05E-06	3.00E-05	3.11E-07	3,421.8	1.03E-01	96.36	95.40	1.39E-02	8.86E-02	86.4%
1.0E-03	4.19E-09	4.19E-06	4.11E-05	3.45E-07	5,215.4	2.14E-01	118.96	117.77	2.91E-02	1.85E-01	86.4%

Table A1.1 – Raindrop distance to maximum velocity

The distance x is the height through which a spherical raindrop of radius r (measured in metres) must fall through air to achieve 99% of its terminal velocity. In each case 86.4% of the change in Potential Energy of the raindrop in travelling distance x to reach its terminal velocity, is used to cut through the air resistance, irrespective of its radius.

We can see from the table that a tiny raindrop with a radius r = 0.1 mm would reach 99% of its terminal velocity $0.99xV_{TERMINAL}$ = 1.18m/s = 2.64 mph after falling just 0.52 metres.

A raindrop with a radius of r = 0.5mm would reach 99% of its terminal velocity after falling 326 metres.

0.99 x $V_{TERMINAL}$ = 29.44 m/s which is 65.9 mph

The average raindrop has a radius of r = 1.0mm A raindrop of this size reaches 99% of its terminal velocity

0.99 x $V_{TERMINAL}$ = 117.77 m/s which is equivalent to 263 mph.

To do this it has to fall through a distance of 5,215.4 metres i.e. more than 5.2 km (~3.24 miles).

Plotting the distance x that raindrops of radius r must fall through in our atmosphere to achieve 99% of their terminal velocity is shown in the graph shown below.

This graph shows that;

$$x = 5.22 \times 10^{15} \, r^4 \quad \dots \text{A1.18}$$

where x and r are both measured in metres.

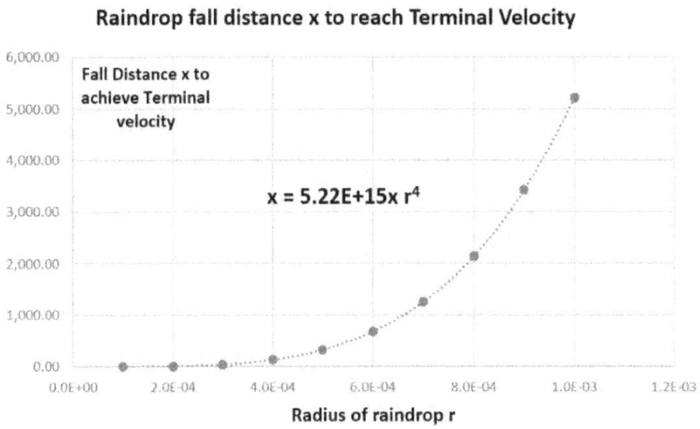

Raindrop fall distance x to reach Terminal Velocity

Graph A1.1 - Distance raindrops reach terminal velocity

The distance x in metres that raindrops of radius r (also in metres) must fall through air in our atmosphere to reach 99% of their terminal velocity $V_o = 0.99 \times V_{TERMINAL}$ calculated by assuming the raindrops remain spherical throughout.

Stop The Storms

Appendix 2 – The Maximum Possible Impact Of Rain

No one is denying that rainfall is a blessing and is absolutely essential to us all, in order to ensure farmers and horticulturists can produce bountiful crops to sustain and nourish us all and so that all of the natural world, both plants and animals, can continue to survive. But there is the possibility that excessive, localised rainfall could contribute to the generation of super-storms. The aim of this calculation is to establish a maximum upper limit on the worst-case scenario for the heating of the atmosphere by rain.

As throughout this work, a number of important assumptions will be made, with a view to simplify the calculations performed. Suppose we consider a typical cloud that exists at a height of 1,500 metres above the ground. Let's assume this drops raindrops, all of which have a radius of exactly one millimetre, and that this rain continues to fall unabated to produce the global annual rainfall of one metre of rain over the period of a year. Let's assume one hundred percent of the potential energy released, goes into heating the column of air immediately below the cloud and that this air does not move in anyway over the course of the entire year. The air does not rise in anyway and it doesn't radiate heat or heat the raindrops or lose heat in any other way. Of course this is totally unrealistic, but it will serve to establish a very approximate, worst-case scenario in terms of falling rain heating the atmosphere.

In the diagram below, a column of air with a cross-sectional area of $1m^2$ is depicted. It has a height of 1,500 metres and stretches up to a cloud which drops enough raindrops to cause the average global annual rainfall of 1 metre over the course of a year. It's assumed all the potential energy of the falling rain goes directly into heating the static column of air.

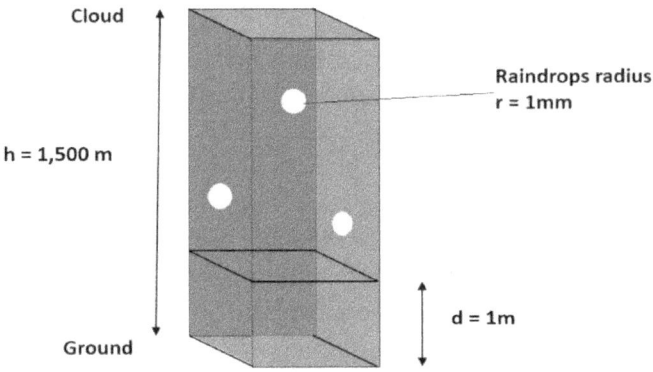

Diagram A2.1 – Air heated by falling rain.

The mass of rain which falls M_w is;

$M_w = V_w \times \rho_w$ ... A2.1

where V_w is the volume of water $V_w = 1m^3$ and the density of water ρ_w = 1,000 kg/m³

So the mass of water M_w = 1,000 kg (one metric tonne)

The Potential Energy released is;-

$PE = M_w \times g \times h$

$PE = 1,000 \times 9.81 \times 1,500 = 1.472 \times 10^7$ Joules ...A2.2

The volume of air in the column;-

$V_{AIR} = 1500 \times 1 = 1,500 \, m^3$ ... A2.3

The mass of air M_{AIR} in the column is given by;-

$M_{AIR} = \rho_{AIR} \times Vol_{AIR} = 1.225 \times 1500 = 1.838 \times 10^3$ ... A2.4

If all the Potential Energy went into heating the column of air then;-

$$PE = M_{AIR} \times SHC_{AIR} \times \Delta T \quad \dots \text{A2.5}$$

where $SHC_{AIR} = 993 \text{ Jkg}^{-1}\text{K}^{-1}$ is the Specific Heat Capacity SHC of air and ΔT is the maximum possible increase in temperature of the column of air.

Therefore, putting the value for the Specific Heat Capacity of air into equation A2.5 and substituting the value for PE from A2.2 we can deduce the worst-case scenario...

$$\Delta T = 8.065 \text{ Kelvin} \quad \dots \text{A2.6}$$

This might not sound very significant, but given that the average global temperature has increased by 1.1°c since 1880 (which is exactly the same as an increase of 1.1 Kelvin) and this is already causing havoc, and the rate of increase has increased to 0.2°c per decade and is set to accelerate even faster, then a temperature increase of this amount would be very significant indeed.

Of course this is a massive overestimate. The column of air wouldn't stay static; the density of warm air generally decreases so it tends to rise and we couldn't expect all the energy from the falling rain to go directly into heating the atmosphere. But it does possibly suggest there might just be some meaningful opportunity to intervene in the rainfall process to some degree, to afford some level of control over the rapid generation of massive, catastrophic storm events.

There is however an additional factor which could be added to this calculation. In common with almost every other substance, water needs energy to change phase from a solid to a liquid or a liquid to a vapour. We call this latent heat – in the case of changing phase from liquid to a gas/vapour we call it *latent heat of vaporisation*.

For water, the latent heat of vaporisation L is very high compared to most other substances. It is given by;-

$$L = 2.261 \times 10^6 \text{ Joules per kg (at 273K)}$$

For the 1,000kg of water that we have discussed above this means an additional 2.261×10^9 Joules of energy is released by the rain as it condenses out of a cloud into liquid rain. *This is nearly 154 times greater than the energy released by the loss of Potential Energy from the 1,000 kg of rain falling from a height of 1,500 metres.*

Clearly this is very significant and is likely to add significantly to the heating of the atmosphere, especially in a critical event like a tornado, where vast amounts of water are being cycled into the atmosphere at an astonishingly fast rate.

Appendix 3 – The Greenhouse Effect

According to Wein's Displacement law, the wavelength at which maximum energy is emitted by any object is related to its temperature T measured in Kelvin by the formula;-

$$\lambda_{max} \times T = K_{WEIN} \quad ... \text{A3.1}$$

where

λ_{max} is the wavelength of peak radiation

and

K_{WEIN} is Wein's constant which is 2.898×10^{-3} m K

Carbon dioxide is an important greenhouse gas. In particular it absorbs and re-emits infrared radiation at two specific infrared frequencies. The two wavelengths are;

4.26 μm and 14.99 μm

Energy of a photon is given by;-

$$E = hf \quad ... \text{A3.2}$$

where h is Planck's constant.

The speed of light c is related to the frequency f and the equivalent wavelength λ by the formula;-

$$c = f \times \lambda \quad ... \text{A3.3}$$

Therefore, the equivalent frequency f related to the infrared absorption wavelengths is given by;-

$$f = c/\lambda \quad ... \text{A3.4}$$

Equation A3.2 can then be used to calculate the equivalent energy E.

The temperature which relates to these peak energy emissions is given by Wein's Displacement law given in equation A3.1

Wavelength λ/m	Frequency f/Hz	Energy E/Joules	Temperature T/Kelvin	°c Celsius
4.26×10^{-6}	7.04×10^{13}	4.66×10^{-20}	680	407
14.99×10^{-6}	2.00×10^{13}	1.33×10^{-20}	193	-80

Table A3.1 - CO_2 Absorption Wavelengths

However, these aren't the only specific infrared wavelengths absorbed and scattered again. Carbon dioxide absorbs radiation across a broad range of infrared wavelengths particularly in the vicinity of these peak absorptions.

Having a temperature averaging[29][30] around 288 Kelvin (about 15°c) the Earth principally emits *infrared radiation* in contrast to the sun which has a surface temperature of about 5,500°c and therefore largely emits *visible light*. It is this contrast in temperature that makes the greenhouse effect so impactful.

P.J. Naughton

Appendix 4 – Controlling Precipitation

Hurricane Helene[11] generated an astonishing amount of precipitation. In total, it is estimated that this storm produced somewhere in the region of 40 trillion gallons of rain. There are 3.78541 litres in a US gallon, so this equates to some 1.51416×10^{14} litres (one litre has a mass of about 1kg).

Large numbers like this defy imagination and are beyond everyday comprehension for most of us. Florida[16] is a big state, it is home to some 23 million people. This amount of rainfall amounts to about 6,580 tonnes of rain per Florida resident. The amount of latent energy required to convert this amount of liquid rain back to vapour (without any change in temperature) would be about 3.434×10^{20} Joules given the Latent Heat of Vaporisation of water is 2.26×10^6 J/kg. This is more than 3.6 times the amount of energy consumed by the whole of the United States each year (~94 exajoules ~ 9.4×10^{19} Joules)

The average rate of energy arriving on the surface of the Earth from the sun[18] is about 342 Watts/m^2 taken over the planet as a whole, which means the amount of energy arriving from the sun each day is 29.5×10^6 Joules per square metre. Solar energy normal to the sun's rays is as high as 1,400 Watts per m^2 but of course the sun never stops moving with respect to any point on Earth and does not stay directly overhead for long.

Using the average rate of the sun's energy arriving on Earth, *the area that would need to be covered with perfect 100% mirrors to reflect the amount of sunlight back into the clouds to reverse this amount of precipitation in one day would be about 1.162×10^{13} m^2* i.e. we'd need to cover a square whose sides were 2,273 miles long with perfect reflectors. If we allowed this energy to be collected over a 5-day period, the area of reflectors required could be reduced to a square with sides of length about 1,016 miles.

This serves to illustrate the extent of the challenge. The Gulf of Mexico stretches about 1,600 km east to west and has a length of about 900km north to south. In total, it covers an area of 1.44×10^{12} m^2 This means we'd need to cover an area about 8.1 times bigger than the size of the whole of the Gulf of Mexico with perfect mirrors to have any hope of *reversing* the total amount of precipitation produced by a hurricane like Helene, within a single day.

65

Stop The Storms

Of course, such a venture would be totally impractical. For a start the cost would be astronomical, not only for purchasing and constructing and installing the reflectors but also for purchasing a suitable plot of land to install them on and for cleaning and maintaining them.

That said, there might be some mileage in the use of portable high energy lasers to help moderate the most extreme local catastrophic buildup of storms but clearly given the energy requirements alone, use of any grid powered device to fully reverse the condensation process in a large scale storm such as storm Helene, is totally impractical due to current energy generation limitations, although this might change at some point if the full extent of the capabilities of nuclear fusion or similar technologies are ever realised.

Nuclear fusion technology in particular, offers enormous promise for meeting our future energy needs. This of course, is the mechanism which powers the sun and all the other stars in the universe. Under enormous pressure at the core of the sun, nuclei of hydrogen atoms are fused together to form helium. As part of this process, a very small part of the mass of the hydrogen nuclei is converted into energy, but given the relationship between mass and energy derived by Einstein's famous formula $E = mc^2$, the amount of energy released in this process is vast.

Deployment of this technology is gradually being developed here on Earth. It will eventually help us to generate clean energy and move away from our current ongoing reliance on fossil fuels, the burning of which generate such massive amounts of harmful greenhouse gases.

However, we should be careful with the use of energy produced by nuclear fusion or any other similar process. If it genuinely delivers the very low-cost energy that is promised, then *we will need to ensure we are not over profligate with the use of this power*.

The climate change issues we are facing are caused by *warming of our climate*. Whilst it's true nuclear fusion won't generate greenhouse gases, it's the warming of our atmosphere that leads to such extreme weather events - storm chaos, flooding and melting of the icecaps. Eventually, nearly all energy ends up in the atmosphere in one form or another.

It is very important that we stop producing greenhouse gases and look to remove these pollutants to reduce global warming, but it's equally important that we learn to control our use of energy and manage our environment sensibly. *We'll be no better off* if, having

66

eliminated excessive production of greenhouse gases, we end up excessively heating the atmosphere with the profligate use of cheap nuclear generated energy instead.

Stop The Storms

P.J. Naughton

Appendix 5 – Preventing Precipitation

This calculation is similar to the calculation performed in appendix 4, but this time instead of calculating the energy required to *reverse precipitation*, converting liquid rain back to a vapour, this time a calculation is made to estimate the energy that would be required to keep the water vapour just 1°c above the dew point and thus avoid precipitation altogether.

As calculated in appendix 4, the amount of precipitation involved in Hurricane Helene amounted to 40 trillion gallons of rain which equates to a mass m = 1.51416 x 10^{14} kg of water. The Specific Heat Capacity of water vapour is SHC_w = 2,020 Jkg^{-1}K^{-1} at 373K

This means the energy E required to increase the temperature of water vapour by 1°c (the same as ΔT = 1 Kelvin) is given by;

$E = m \times SHC_W \times \Delta T$ ... A5.1

Therefore, the energy required to keep this amount of water vapour 1°c above the dew point would be;-

$E = 3.059 \times 10^{17}$ Joules   ... A5.2

Although this is an improvement on the amount of energy required to reverse this amount of precipitation calculated in appendix 4, this is still an astoundingly high level of energy, amounting to about 0.325% of the annual energy consumption of the USA.

The area of land that would need to be used to reflect this amount of energy from the sun over a 5-day period assuming 100% reflectivity, would amount to about 2.07x10^9 m^2

This equates to 920 square miles so would need a piece of land about 30.3 miles by 30.3 miles. This is perhaps more achievable. If this could be done at a cost of say 1$ per square metre (which is probably the lowest possible cost) it would require an investment of at least $2.07 billion dollars. This is a substantial investment but compared to the $88 billion damage caused by Helene, it might be something worth considering.

Stop The Storms

There would of course be considerable challenges in attempting to implement this kind of strategy. There's no guarantee this approach would provide the effective level of protection required. For a start, it would be difficult to control the equitable delivery of energy to ensure energy was spread equally, so that every gram of water vapour was warmed at least by the required amount.

There's also immense difficulty in trying to predict the exact location where storms are likely to germinate, and the exact path which they are likely to follow as they develop. Many such events begin life many thousands of miles away out in the Pacific or from distant reaches of the Atlantic. Designing an array of reflectors on this scale that could be sufficiently mobile to move to the required location, fast enough to eliminate impending storms in worsening weather conditions, would be a massive engineering challenge, difficult in the extreme.

There would no doubt be plenty of other challenges associated with a strategy of this kind. For example, making sure such a large array of reflectors remained 100% effective wouldn't be easy and it's more than likely gathering storm clouds would significantly reduce the amount of sunlight reaching the reflectors, thus reducing their effectiveness. Also, the array of reflectors would need to be sufficiently robust to withstand the repeated ravishing by severe storms. Even so, a solution of this kind would probably be worthy of further consideration.

Appendix 6 – Temperature Varies With Height

When an amount of gas with mass m rises through height h it gains Potential Energy given by ;-

$$PE = mgh \quad \text{... A6.1}$$

Where g is the acceleration due to gravity. g will decrease with height, but we can assume it remains almost constant near the Earth's surface at g = 9.81 m/s^2

If the temperature of the gas falls by temperature ΔT, the energy lost E is given by;-

$$E = m \times SHC \times \Delta T \quad \text{... A6.2}$$

Where SHC is the Specific Heat Capacity of the gas. If all the gain in Potential Energy comes from cooling the gas, from A6.1 and A6.2 we can say;-

$$mgh = m \times SHC \times \Delta T \quad \text{... A6.3}$$

Therefore ...

$$\Delta T = gh/SHC \quad \text{... A6.4}$$

The Specific Heat Capacity SHC of air is 993 J/kg/°c

This gives a temperature drop of about 0.99°c for every 100 metres of height.
The actual drop in temperature with height varies depending on climatic conditions but in the U.K. it's generally about 0.5°c for every 100 metres of vertical height.

Stop The Storms

Appendix 7 – Deflecting Winds

It is interesting to investigate to what extent it might be possible to deflect the winds of a storm up into the atmosphere. Suppose the horizontal wind speed is V and a sample of air has mass m such that the Kinetic Energy of this sample would be;-

$$KE = \tfrac{1}{2} mV^2 \quad ... A7.1$$

Suppose a barrier is placed in the way of this sample of wind so it's deflected vertically as shown in the diagram below.

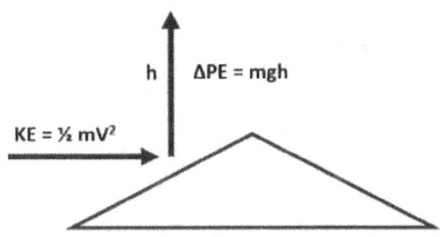

Diagram A7.1 – Diverting Gale Force Winds

If all the Kinetic Energy of our sample were converted to Potential Energy then it would reach height h where;

$$PE = mgh = KE \quad ... A7.2$$

A7.1 & A7.2 =>

$$h = V^2/2g \quad ... A7.3$$

Storm Helene had a sustained wind speed of about 140 mph which equates to...

$$V = 58.33 \text{ m/s}$$

Plugging this into equation A7.3 gives a maximum height h of 173.43metres. However, we couldn't expect the conversion of energy to be 100% There'd be energy "loss" in terms of heat and sound. We could probably expect the same sort of percentage energy required to overcome air resistance to be similar to the value derived in appendix 1 (86%) for the falling raindrops.

So, with only 14% of kinetic energy converted to potential energy, the maximum height reached by the diverted air would probably be nearer h = 24.3 metres. Whilst this might prove of some use to help protect low rise properties at least to some limited extent, it probably wouldn't do much to raise the cloud base in anyway whatsoever. Care should be taken not to think of this as offering the same level of protection as a solid wall of a similar height. This kind of ramp might deflect the wind upwards, but the vertical wind speed would only be a fraction of the horizontal wind speed and would rapidly decrease with height, so the protection offered would only ever be very minimal indeed. Also, it might not prove tremendously helpful if it caused the wind to push up against a roof that wasn't designed to take this kind of resultant upward force.

With a wind speed of *only* V = 100 mph (still a massive wind speed but perhaps a more typical value in major storm events) using the same assumptions, the height reached would only be about 12.4 metres – about half the value calculated for the 140mph wind speed.

All in all, this means the deflection idea is only of very limited value. Of course, it might be possible to design some kind of large U bend pipe that might be able to reverse the prevailing wind and push directly against it. This might be of some use and offer a limited degree of protection to local residences, but it's unlikely it would be useful to provide widescale protection in any meaningful way.

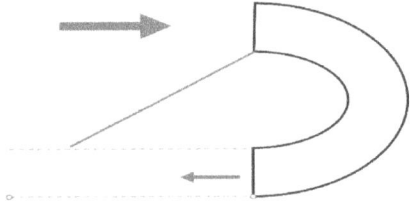

Diagram A7.2 – Pushing the Wind Back.

Appendix 8 – Desalination

The Gulf of Mexico is thought to contain about 2.4×10^{18} kg of sea water. The salt levels in this area are roughly similar to the Atlantic at about 36 parts per 1,000.

Sea water has a lower Specific Heat Capacity than fresh water.

$SHC_{SEA\ WATER}$ = 3,900 J/Kg/Kelvin

The surface temperature of oceans is widely thought to be critical in the process of generating major storms. Once this temperature reaches about 26.5°c the risk of a hurricane being generated becomes severe. This temperature equates roughly to about 300 Kelvin.

For the sake of argument, let's assume the average temperature in the Gulf of Mexico is about 286 Kelvin – approximately midway between 0°c and 26.5°c This is only a very rough approximation but it's probably accurate enough for general estimation purposes.

The total heat energy in the waters of the Gulf would be given by...

$E = m \times SHC \times T$ ... A8.1

This gives an estimate for the total heat energy in the water to be;

$E = 2.68 \times 10^{24}$ Joules

If this water was fresh water instead of salt water the Specific Heat Capacity would be 7.4% higher.

$SHC_{FRESH\ WATER}$ = 4,190 J/kg/Kelvin

We can plug this value into equation A8.1 to calculate the average temperature that we'd have for the same amount of energy if all the water in the Gulf were converted to fresh water.

The equivalent temperature would be 266 Kelvin almost 20°c cooler. Of course, this value is artificially too low as this is below freezing (0°c)

Stop The Storms

but hopefully it serves to illustrate just how much impact desalination could actually have.

Total desalination would be a major exercise and would not be desirable as it would no doubt have a serious adverse ecological impact on marine flora and fauna. However, if we could reduce the salt levels in the Gulf by just 5% the average surface temperature would drop *by at least* an estimated 1.1°c

This might not sound like much but the impact this would have on suppressing major storms would be extremely significant.

There are also some additional potential bonuses to be gained from this approach;-

i. Although the Gulf of Mexico is over 1,300 miles from the equator, it is located in a very warm part of the globe. There are no official deserts on its shores as such, but there are large regions of arid scrub land in the near vicinity. It might be possible to utilise some of these areas to naturally desalinate sea water, utilising intense rays of heat from the sun to evaporate the water to leave the salt (sodium chloride) residue behind. This would be relatively easy to setup and there would be an additional small dividend as the reflectivity of the shiny white salt crystals would be something in the order of 10% or thereabouts, so at least some of the sun's light could be reflected back into space, thus slightly reducing the greenhouse effect.

It would be advantageous to locate this operation in an area that would not increase the presence of water vapour in the area of the Gulf, taking into account the prevailing winds, but this ought to be reasonably easy to achieve. It has the added benefit that it would require only a fairly moderate investment, plus the 'table salt' by-product would have a substantial commercial value which could offset the costs involved.

ii. There is another benefit which might also be worthy of note. *The density of freshwater is actually lower than the density of sea water.* This is a rare win-win. This means that the cooling freshwater, with its higher Specific Heat Capacity, should in theory tend to float towards the upper strata of the sea – thus further reducing the all-important surface temperature of the ocean.

76

Freshwater does boil at a temperature 4°c lower than seawater (100°c v 104°c) so would tend to evaporate more readily, but this 4% setback is not thought to be sufficient to cancel out the gain from the 7.4% increase in Specific Heat Capacity and also the reflectivity of sunlight (albedo) is much greater for freshwater compared to seawater, so the greenhouse effect would overall be reduced.

The Evaporation of Brine

A simple experiment was performed to compare the rates of evaporation of brine and fresh tap water. Four test-tubes were filled with water – two with fresh tap water and two with fully saturated brine (a mixture of tap water and table salt). The test-tubes were then left in a laboratory at room temperature (varying between 10°c and 21°c). Four test tubes were used for this experiment in total - two contained saturated brine and two contained fresh water. This was done to check that the results were consistent between different types of test-tube. One set of test-tubes had a green glass tint, whilst the other pair had an orange tint. Both a green and an orange test-tube was used for both brine and for fresh water. As a starting position, the test-tubes were filled to the absolute brim with their respective liquids.

After exactly two weeks (14 days – measured to within one hour), each test-tube had lost a considerable amount of its water through evaporation, but *there was no significant difference* observed in the heights of the water measured across the four test-tubes (see photograph below).

This is *not* a fully comprehensive representation of the differences that might be observed in the oceans between **Brine (B)** and **Freshwater (F)** as it does *not* take into account any effects that might be caused by winds, wave action and other the mechanics of other weather-related processes. However, it does strongly suggest that the slightly elevated boiling point of brine compared to freshwater (377 Kelvin brine v 373 Kelvin freshwater – a difference of 4 Kelvin == 4°c) would not necessarily prove to be a major setback to the proposal being made to reduce the heating of seawater through a technique of desalination, thus slightly increasing the Specific Heat Capacity of the ocean waters.

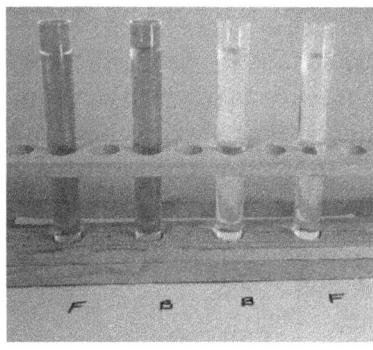

Photograph A8.1 – Evaporation Brine (B) v Freshwater (F)

Brine has a higher density than fresh water. Pure water has a density of 998 kg/m³ whilst seawater has a density of 1,025 kg/m³ However freshwater has a much higher Specific Heat Capacity. This experiment suggests that if desalination could help to control the excessive heating of the ocean, the lowering of the boiling point of the desalinated waters in the upper layer of the oceans would not necessarily lead to increased evaporation that would otherwise increase the amount of precipitation in the atmosphere.

The location and seasonal utilisation of desalination plants would need be carefully calculated, but if they could increase the steady supply of cooling fresh water rainfall into places like the Mexican Gulf, in a timely fashion without increasing the incidence of greenhouse gas water vapour in the atmosphere, then the results could be enormously beneficial for everyone in and around the area.

One possible further improvement to this solution would be to capture water vapour at the desalination plants and pipe it directly into the Gulf, thereby minimising any significant increase in water vapour in the upper atmosphere and avoiding any greenhouse warming this might otherwise cause.

The exact details would need to be carefully worked out to maximize the benefits of this solution, but the potential benefits are enormous and the achievable investments required make this potentially an extremely attractive proposition.

Appendix 9 – Land for Desalination

As stated in appendix 8, the Gulf of Mexico[17] is thought to contain about 2.4 x 10^{18} kg of sea water. In appendix 4 the average rate of energy arriving on the surface of the Earth from the sun was quoted at about 342 Watts/m^2 taken over the planet as a whole, which means the average energy arriving from the sun each day is somewhere in the region of 29.5 x10^6 Joules per square metre. The peak power is much higher than this, but we are only interested in an average rate, although in places nearer to the equator where Florida is located, this value is likely to be significantly higher.

Let's assume that all this energy goes into converting water from liquid water to vapour i.e. it is all used as latent heat of vaporisation. This will not be entirely correct, some of the heat would likely go into raising the temperature of the liquid water, but this calculation will hopefully provide a reasonable best-case scenario.

It would be relatively easy to re-work the calculation to include the energy required to raise the temperature of seawater say from 20°c to 100°c. But this wouldn't necessarily provide an accurate answer either as water can and does evaporate at temperatures well below 100°c.

Using the assumption that all the solar energy E arriving in a square metre converts to latent energy in time t we can say;

$$E/At = m \times L/At \qquad ... A9.1$$

where E/At = 342 Watts/m^2 and L is the Latent Heat of vaporization of water which is L = 2.261 x10^6 J/kg

Therefore in 1 hour (3,600 seconds) the maximum amount of water evaporated by solar energy landing on one square metre would be roughly;-

$$m = (342 \times 3600)/2.261x10^6 \qquad ... A9.2$$

$$m = 0.545 \text{ kg} \qquad ... A9.3$$

Stop The Storms

There are 175,200 hours in 20 years, so roughly, over this timescale, at best we might hope for 95,403 kg of water to be evaporated by each square metre of land. 5% of the entire mass of water in the Gulf of Mexico would be 1.2×10^{17} kg

So, the area of land required to evaporate this amount of water in a 20-year period would be at least 1.26×10^{12} square metres which equals an area of land about 750 miles long and 750 miles wide - some 559,032 square miles. By any reckoning, this is a very substantial amount of real estate. However, the land required would not need to be prime grade agricultural land - scrub land or desert would be ideal.

There aren't any deserts as such in the state of Florida, but there are some arid regions of substantial size located in areas further west. The Chihuahuan Desert[21], for example, covers an extensive area of more than 190,000 square miles, stretching from Mexico into the southern states of Arizona, New Mexico and Texas. This might make an ideal location to establish a large scale, solar powered desalination plant to satisfy about 33% of this requirement.

Channelling the water from the Gulf of Mexico to such areas would undoubtedly pose a challenge, but given the potential benefits, this should not be unsurmountable. Perhaps the construction of a canal or a large-scale pipeline would be the most ideal solution. Clearly, infrastructure on this scale would require some substantial investment, but the potential benefits are truly enormous. Not only would the incidence of massive tropical cyclones be reduced in the region, but also the by-product of salt, thought to be present in the Gulf in the ratio at about 36 parts per 1,000 would be produced.

P.J. Naughton

Appendix 10 – Heat Conduction in the Sea

The *maximum* power of the radiation arriving on the surface of the Earth from the sun when the sun is directly overhead and the radiation is therefore at normal incidence (90 degrees) is about 1,400 Watts/m^2 This is the peak value. The average value[18] is about 342 Watts/m^2 measured over the globe as a whole.

We know from Stefan-Boltzmann's law that a perfect radiator with a temperature T measured in Kelvins, will radiate energy at the rate of;

$$P/A = \sigma T^4 \quad ... A10.1$$

where σ is Stefan's constant which is σ = 5.6696 x 10^{-8} Wm^{-2}K^{-4} So, at a surface temperature of 27°c (300.16 Kelvin) the radiation from the surface of a perfect radiating sea would be about...

$$P/A = 460.17 \text{ W/m}^2 \quad ...A10.2$$

This is 32.87% of the *maximum* radiation arriving from the sun, although it's also 34.55% greater than the *average* radiation arriving from the sun.

The table below shows the amount of radiation from each square metre of the Earth at various surface temperatures (assuming the Earth to be a perfect radiator). Even at 0°c the Earth would re-radiate about 92.29% of the average radiation which arrives from the sun. At the very high temperature of 123.26°c the Earth would radiate as much energy from its surface as the *maximum* energy arriving from the sun, but of course this temperature would be far too high to sustain life as we know it.

T /°c	T/K	T^4	P/A = σT^4	% of MAX	% of AVERAGE
0	273.16	5.568E+09	315.63	22.54%	92.29%
15	288.16	6.895E+09	390.88	27.92%	114.29%
27	300.16	8.117E+09	460.17	32.87%	134.55%
123.26	396.42	2.470E+10	1400.00	100.00%	409.36%

Table A10.1 – Energy Radiated By Hot Surfaces

Stop The Storms

At best, with 460.17 Watts/m² being radiated by the surface of the sea at a temperature of 27°c we'd still have to deal with somewhere in the region of 1,000 Watts/m² to prevent sea water temperatures climbing higher during periods when peak amounts of radiation were arriving from the sun.

One possible way that heat might be moved away from the surface of the sea is by *conduction downwards*. However, water is not a good conductor. If we consider a column of water of area 1m² and depth 700 metres with a temperature at one end of 27°c and a temperature at the other end of 6°c (similar to values we might observe in columns of seawater in warmer climes) then we can calculate the rated of energy conducted away from the surface;-

$$P = K_{SEA} \times A \times \Delta T/h \quad ...A10.3$$

where K_{SEA} is the Thermal Conductivity of seawater $K_{SEA} = 0.591$ Wm⁻¹K⁻¹ and the temperature difference ΔT between the top and bottom of the column is 21 Kelvin and the cross-sectional area A = 1m² as shown in the diagram below.

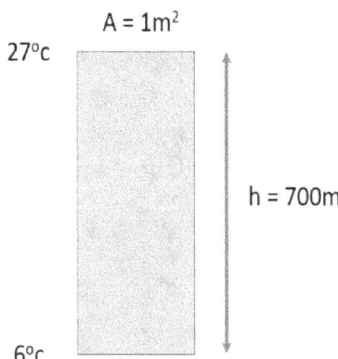

Diagram A10.1 – Energy Conducted through Seawater

The power *conducted* through this column of water, assuming no disturbance caused by waves or convection currents ..etc. would be...

$$P/A = 0.0177 \text{ Watts/m}^2 \quad ...A10.4$$

which is clearly way below the ~1,000 Watts/m^2 needed to prevent the surface of the water heating any further above 27°c

Even if we put a column of an extremely good conductor such as aluminium in place (the coefficient of Thermal Conductivity for aluminium K_{AL} = 201 W/m^{-1}K^{-1}) we'd need a cross-sectional area of about 175m^2 to conduct this amount of excess energy away from a *single square metre* of the surface down to a depth of 700 metres with a temperature difference of only 21°c between top and bottom. This assumes no heat loss through the sides, so in reality we'd likely achieve a better level of cooling than this simple calculation would suggest, but still nowhere near the level required. At an approximate cost of ~£1,500 per metric tonne, a single column of this magnitude would cost somewhere in the region of £615 million (about $780 million U.S. dollars) which is clearly an *impractical proposition* given this would only provide a solution for a *single square metre* of ocean.

Stop The Storms

Appendix 11 – Pumping Cold Seawater

Even in tropical climates, cold sea water exists deep down in the sea as long as the water is deep enough. At a depth of about 700 metres, sea water is generally found to be at a temperature not much in excess of about 6°c

We might wonder, *how much of this water could be pumped to the surface if we could utilise the maximum amount of the sun's energy?*

The water would need to be given Potential Energy PE where...

$$PE = mgh \qquad \text{... A11.1}$$

where m is the mass of water, g is the acceleration due to gravity g= 9.81 m/s^2 and h is the height raised, which we'll assume for the purposes of this calculation is 700 metres.

Assuming that we could build a machine that was 100% efficient, which is obviously not possible but we'll assume for the sake of simplicity this could be the case, then with energy arriving at the rate of 1400 Joules per second...

$$1400 = (m/t) \times 9.81 \times 700 \qquad \text{... A11.2}$$

The mass per second that we could raise would therefore be about 0.204 kg per second. Over an hour this would amount to about 734kg which, given the density of sea water is about 1,025 kg/m^3 would be sufficient to fill a column of water of area one square metre to a depth of about 0.716 metres. Assuming that on nett, after taking into account the heat, mainly infrared, radiated from the surface of the warm sea, that only about 1,000 Watts of radiant energy from the sun is absorbed exclusively by this water, then its temperature would increase by about 1.26°c every hour.

But this would still only leave it at 7.26°c if some way could be found to keep it undispersed and intact at the surface. If this water were spread out to a theoretical depth of 4.5cm (and again isolated from dispersion in some way), its temperature would be increased by the absorption of 1,000 Watts/m^2 by about 20°c in a single hour, leaving it at a temperature of some 26°c. However, this means that the area that this amount of water would cover, would still only prove to be a fairly modest 15.9 square metres.

The number of machines that would be required to make even a tiny impression on the excessive heating of the surface of the oceans in this way would be vast. Unfortunately, there is nothing to be gained in terms of improved cooling by pumping water from less depth. What gains could be made in terms of using solar power to pump *greater volumes of water* to the surface through *less height*, would be more than lost in terms of the higher temperatures in the shallower waters.

Of course, as previously mentioned storms generate very high winds. It might be the case that the considerable energy in these very strong winds could be used in some way to cool the surface of the sea by pumping cold waters up from the depths, but this would likely be somewhat very late in the lifecycle of the gestation of any storm. Whether this could ever be a realistic proposition is difficult to say. Certainly, the costs incurred resulting from damage to property caused by severe storms can in many cases be extremely high, not to mention the suffering caused by the loss of homes, terrible injury and the tragic loss of life, which in all too many cases are truly catastrophic. However, the sheer scale of the vast areas that are at risk of severe storm generation are such that it would be extremely difficult and very costly to build sufficient cooling facilities to provide sufficient widescale protection. A solution of this kind might be of use in some specific local areas where there is a clearly defined high risk of the frequent occurrence of particularly severe storms, but in general, this just doesn't seem either practical or cost effective.

In any case, this kind of solution does have some limitations. It relies on cold water being readily available at depth. But in the case of some parts of the sea, this just doesn't prove to be the case. Take for example the Gulf of Mexico[17]. This is a vast piece of ocean, extending over some 620,000 square miles. It has a maximum depth of some 4,384 metres and on average, at 1,615 metres, it's more than a mile deep. However, 32% of its area stands on the Continental shelf, and as such, this large section only has a depth of some 500 feet (about 152 metres). In these locations, its depth is well short of the 700-metre depth thought necessary to achieve the low temperatures that would otherwise exist in much deeper waters. As such, the colder waters that would be needed to cool the surface just aren't available in the quantities required to move the dial and make a substantial difference to the overheating of the surface. Some other solution has to be found.

Stop The Storms

Appendix 12 – Breaking Clouds

There is strong evidence to suggest that storm clouds breakup and give up the massive content of water they have gathered, when they come into contact with other opposite electrically charged clouds, thereby effectively "losing" their charge. It is very likely that this will provide a very cost-effective solution for forcing major storm clouds to divulge their contents prematurely over sea and breakup before they reach land where, when left unmanaged, they often cause disaster due to extreme flooding.

The average *electric charge* (Q) of a thundercloud is well documented[31],[32],[33],[34],[35] In general, a typical thundercloud carries anything between 10 Coulombs and 100 Coulombs of charge. For the sake of this calculation, I'll assume a typical value of somewhere in the region Q = 50 Coulombs

The voltage of a thundercloud has also been measured[36] The voltage V is as high as;-

$$V = 1.3 \, GVolts \quad \ldots A12.1$$

Using these values we can calculate the average energy in a thundercloud to be;-

$$E = V \times Q = 6.5 \times 10^{10} \, Joules \quad \ldots A12.2$$

This is a vast amount of energy, sufficient to meet the entire energy needs of a typical city for many days.

Suppose we considered discharging the electrical energy from a cloud by use of a wet rope strung through it and reaching all the way down to the ground as illustrated in the diagram below;-

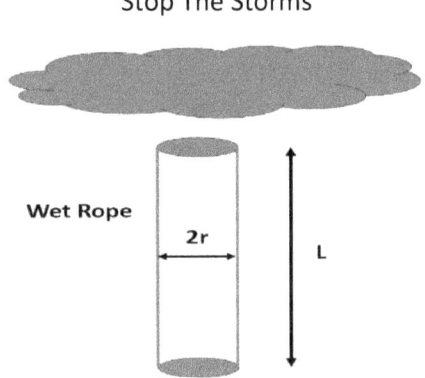

Diagram A12.1 – Rope Hung From Cloud

A length of wet rope length L and radius r is hung from a thundercloud. The Resistance R of the rope can be calculated from;-

$$R = \rho_r \times L / A \qquad \ldots A12.3$$

where ρ_r is the electrical resistivity of the wet rope. The resistivity of the wet rope would in effect be the resistivity of water. The resistivity of water varies quite markedly[37]...

- Seawater: 0.2 ohm meters ($\Omega \cdot m$)
- Drinking water: 2-200 ($\Omega \cdot m$)
- Deionized water: 180,000 ($\Omega \cdot m$)

Assuming we are using deionized (rainwater) then the resistivity ρ_r would be;

$$\rho_r = 180,000 \ \Omega \cdot m$$

Assuming the average height of the raincloud to be L = 1,500 metres, we can work out the expected resistance R for ropes with different cross sectional areas $A = \pi r^2$ where r is the radius of the rope. From Ohm's law we know the relationship between voltage V, current I and Resistance R;

$$V = I \times R \qquad \ldots A12.4$$

And we know that power P = I x V so we can say...

$$P = V^2/R \quad ... \text{A12.5}$$

where V is the voltage V of the cloud V = 1.3 x10^9 volts

Of course, if the rope is conducting large amounts of electricity, it's likely to get hot. From the Stefan-Boltzmann law it's easy to calculate the temperature T that the rope would need to reach to radiate away *all this power* as heat...

$$P = \sigma T^4 \times A_s \quad ... \text{A12.6}$$

where σ is Stefan's constant, T is the temperature of the rope and A_s is the surface area of the rope where...

$$A_S = 2\pi rL \quad ... \text{A12.7}$$

A table of calculated results is shown below starting with a radius r = 0.5 mm

Radius r/m	$A_c = \pi r^2$	$R = \rho_p x L/A$	$P = V^2/R$	$A_s = 2\pi rL$	$T = (P/\sigma A_s)^{1/4}$	T/°c	M	t = E/P	t/hrs	t/days
0.0005	7.85E-07	3.44E+14	4.92E+03	4.71	368.3	95.2	1.18	13,222,103.0	3,672.8	153.03
0.0010	3.14E-06	8.59E+13	1.97E+04	9.42	438.0	164.8	4.71	3,305,525.7	918.2	38.26
0.0015	7.07E-06	3.82E+13	4.42E+04	14.14	484.7	211.6	10.60	1,469,122.6	408.1	17.00
0.0020	1.26E-05	2.15E+13	7.87E+04	18.85	520.9	247.7	18.85	826,381.4	229.6	9.56
0.0025	1.96E-05	1.38E+13	1.23E+05	23.56	550.8	277.6	29.45	528,884.1	146.9	6.12
0.0030	2.83E-05	9.55E+12	1.77E+05	28.27	576.4	303.3	42.41	367,280.6	102.0	4.25
0.0035	3.85E-05	7.02E+12	2.41E+05	32.99	599.1	325.9	57.73	269,838.8	75.0	3.12
0.0040	5.03E-05	5.37E+12	3.15E+05	37.70	619.4	346.3	75.40	206,595.4	57.4	2.39
0.0045	6.36E-05	4.24E+12	3.98E+05	42.41	637.9	364.8	95.43	163,235.8	45.3	1.89
0.0050	7.85E-05	3.44E+12	4.92E+05	47.12	655.0	381.8	117.81	132,221.0	36.7	1.53

Table A12.1 – Time t to Discharge Cloud

The *wet* rope length 1,500 metres, soaked in de-ionized rain water with radius r has cross sectional area A_c and Resistance R. It has mass M assuming density 1,000 kg/m^3

t is the time taken to discharge the cloud with a single strand of rope.

Stop The Storms

T is the temperature needed to radiate all the energy away as heat and is provided merely to indicate an upper limit on the maximum temperature the rope could theoretically reach.

The second line of this table shows that a rope (really a length of string) with a radius of r= 1mm would transmit 19.7kW of power to the ground and discharge the entire cloud within 38.26 days. In doing so it wouldn't reach a temperature in excess of 164.8°c. In truth, the maximum temperature reached would be much lower than this, as this assumes all the energy would be radiated as heat from the rope.

A rope of this length would not be expensive. In fact, a roll of string with this radius (r = 1mm) is currently available in 100 metre rolls for £3.47p from Amazon. This means we could get 1,500 metres for £52 (about $66 U.S. dollars) Of course having to wait 38 days to discharge a cloud isn't very attractive, but if we had 38 lengths of rope (total cost less than £2,000 which is approximately ~$2,500 U.S. dollars) then it's *estimated* the discharge could be completed in a single day.

The costs involved here are very modest in comparison to the billion-dollar losses frequently incurred by storm damage. Of course, other costs would also need to be taken into account. We'd need some means of suspending the ropes for a start. Possibly a series of drones could be used. Also ropes of different dimensions would be required to deal with bigger/higher clouds and the best process for keeping the strings suitably wet would need to be worked out. But as a general principle, the idea of discharging storm clouds by utilising wet ropes seems an extremely attractive one in terms of cost and logistics, even though it is, to all intents and purposes, a very basic solution.

Careful thought will need to be given to the precise design of the drones utilised for this purpose. A special type of drone will be needed to reach such heights and maintain a good degree of stability in high winds and extreme storm conditions, whilst at the same time ensuring that there's optimum contact between the charges in the cloud and the "earthed" ropes. Care would need to be taken not to impede air traffic corridors.

Similarly, at the lower end, a carefully designed weight would be required to ensure the maximum efficiency of the discharge process and to maintain good electrical contact between the conducting ropes and the sea. It might be possible to optimize the discharge of clouds by devising a hollow, cylindrical design for the rope which might retain more water and thus be more stable and conduct more efficiently.

Perhaps further refinements could be made to this proposal. For example, it might be possible to capture the energy released in this process and make good use of it, possibly to de-carbonize the atmosphere in some way.

It might for example, be desirable to use some of this energy to tackle rising sea-levels. Electrolysis could possibly be used to split quantities of sea water (H_2O) into the component hydrogen and oxygen gases. These could be captured and used as environmentally friendly green fuels. In any event, it seems highly likely *this solution should be considered for implementation* given the potential cost-effective protection it clearly promises to so easily provide.

Stop The Storms

Appendix 13 – Water Droplets

Terminal Velocity

The terminal velocity of a spherical droplet of water falling through air can easily be calculated, if we assume it maintains a spherical shape throughout.

According to Stoke's law, the viscous force F on a spherical object with radius r moving at velocity v through a viscous fluid (gas or liquid) which has a coefficient of viscosity η is given by;-

$$F = 6\pi v r \eta \qquad \dots \text{A13.1}$$

As the object moves with an increased velocity, the size of the viscous force increases in direct proportion. When this resistive force equals the force of gravity pulling the falling object downwards – which we usually refer to as its weight, then the object won't accelerate anymore as the resultant *net* force pulling it downwards will be zero. So, assuming no other external forces are involved, the falling object would be subject to no further acceleration. At this point, the terminal velocity of the object in this viscous medium would have been reached.

It's therefore possible to use the weight F of a spherical object of mass m (where F = mg) to find the terminal velocity it would reach when falling through a viscous medium with a known coefficient of viscosity η.

The diagram below shows the forces involved. The force of gravity pulling the object down towards the ground is the weight of the object. The viscous force acting on the falling object serves to resist its motion, effectively pushing it upwards.

When these two forces equal each other, the net force downwards will become zero and the terminal velocity will have been reached.

Stop The Storms

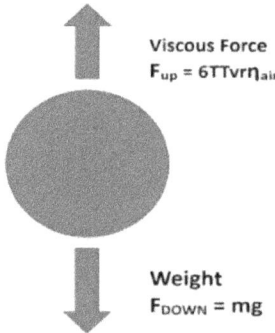

Viscous Force
$F_{up} = 6\pi vr\eta_{air}$

Weight
$F_{DOWN} = mg$

Diagram A13.1 – Viscous Force on falling droplet

Once the viscous force equals the weight, the droplet won't accelerate any further.

Assuming a spherical droplet, the mass is given by…

$$m = 4/3 \times \pi r^3 \times \rho_{water} \qquad … A13.2$$

where the density of water ρ_{water} = 998 kg/m³

With a radius of 10 microns r = 10^{-5} metres therefore the mass m = 4.18 x 10^{-12} kg
Assuming the acceleration due to gravity remains constant at g = 9.81 m/s² and doesn't change significantly with height over the distances involved here, then the downward force, the weight of the droplet, would be…

$$F_{DOWN} = 4.1 \times 10^{-11} \text{ Newtons} \qquad … A13.3$$

Actually, the acceleration due to gravity would of course reduce slightly with height. At a height h of 1,500 metres above the ground, the acceleration due to gravity would be;

$$g = GM/(R+h)^2 \qquad … A13.4$$

where M is the mass of the Earth, R is the radius of the Earth and h is the height above the ground.
The mass of the Earth is M = 5.978 x 10^{24} kg and the Earth's radius R is;

$R = 6.378 \times 10^6$ m

When h = 1,500 metres g would be 0.0046 m/s^2 lower than at ground level i.e. the value of **g would be reduced by about 0.05%** which is not thought to be significant here. At a much greater height, for example h = 15,000 metres (about 10 miles) the reduction in the acceleration due to gravity would still only be about 0.47%

Using equations A13.1 and A13.3 we can say, when the downward force (the weight) equals the viscous force then;-

$4.1 \times 10^{-11} = 6\pi\, V_{TERMINAL}\, r\eta$ ... A13.5

Putting in a value for the radius of the 10 micron droplet r = 10×10^{-6} and the coefficient of viscosity η_{air} = 1.51×10^{-5} Nsm^{-2} we can say;

$V_{TERMINAL}$ = 0.0144 m/s

So, the time t taken for the 10μm droplet to fall distance h to the ground with no other forces at play would be;

$t = h/V$ ... A13.6

This works out to be 1.041 $\times 10^5$ secs or 28.92 hours which is perhaps much longer than we might have expected, based on the absence of any other force. *However, other forces do indeed play a part on the falling droplet.*

The Velocity of Thermal Updrafts

Consider a column of air with a cross-sectional area A = 1m² stretching up above the Earth's surface to height h, as far as our atmosphere reaches.

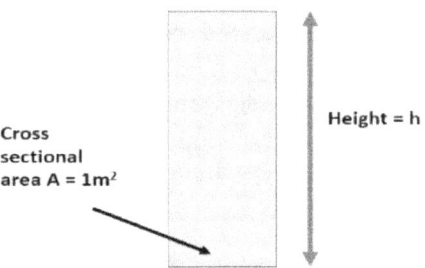

Diagram A13.2 – A column of air with height h

Assuming the density of this column of air ρ_{air} to be constant, the pressure P at the bottom of this column would be;

$P = h\rho_{air}g$ ... A13.7

We know the pressure P at ground level averages 101,325 N/m² and the density of air ρ_{air} at S.T.P. is 1.293 kg/m³ so we can calculate the equivalent height h that this theoretical column of air *with constant density* would need to be, to create this pressure. This comes out to be;

h = 7,988.2 metres

Of course, the density of air would reduce with height as the pressure would be lower at elevated heights, but in the interests of simplicity let us assume this is not the case.

Using this estimated value, we can calculate the mass m of this theoretical column;

m = volume x density ... A13.8

Where volume = height x cross-sectional area A which we are assuming is 1m²

98

So, using the same constant density for air ρ_{air} = 1.293 kg/m³ we can say this theoretical column of air would have mass m = 10,328 kg

The energy E required to lift this entire column through height L would be;

$$E = mgL \quad \text{... A13.9}$$

If we assume the maximum power W of radiation from the sun were used to lift this column we could say;

$$W = E/t = mgL/t \quad \text{... A13.10}$$

where L/t = $V_{UPDRAFT}$ the velocity of the updraft.

Since the maximum power W arriving from the sun incident normal to Earth's surface is W = 1,400 Watts

We can say, if the assumptions made were true, the maximum velocity of the updraft would be;

$$V_{UPDRAFT} = 1400/mg \quad \text{... A13.11}$$

Plugging in the mass of our theoretical column of air m = 10,328 kg we get;-

$$V_{UPDRAFT} = 0.0138 \text{ m/s} \quad \text{... A13.12}$$

Although some big assumptions have been made here which are clearly not in any way entirely correct, this estimate will have some validity in terms of illustrating *the order of magnitude* of the velocity of the updraft, as the same theoretical *equivalent column of air* with a *fixed density* has been used consistently throughout.

Of course, we wouldn't expect any such column of air to move upwards with constant uniform velocity in exactly this way. Nor could we expect the radiation from the sun to be maintained at a maximum value throughout the entire day at any particular fixed point on the planet. Solar radiation of this intensity would only ever reach the surface of the Earth on a clear day, for a short period, whilst ever the sun was directly overhead.

In reality, the dynamics of any such air mass would be very much more complex than has been illustrated in this simplistic calculation, but at least, it's hoped this serves to illustrate the important part the updraft plays in maintaining our delicately balanced weather systems.

P.J. Naughton

Appendix 14 – Electrolysis of Sea Water

In the 30 years between 1993 and 2023 global sea levels rose by 101 millimetres due to the melting of the polar icecaps caused by global warming. This amounted to an average increase of

$h = 3.36$mm per year   ... A14.1

With a density of *freshwater* at about 998 kg/m³ this means the increase in the mass of water in each square metre of ocean surface would be $\Delta m = 3.36$ kg per year. Actually, seawater has a density of 1,025 kg/m³ which would give a mass increase of 3.44 kg per square metre. A rounded value for mass increase will be used here;-

$\Delta m = 3.4$ kg per square metre   ... A14.2

Pure water has a molecular weight of 18 so each mole of water has a mass of 18 grams. This means the increase in water under each squared metre of sea surface would be;

$\Delta V/A = 186.7$ moles per m² per year   ... A14.3

The energy E required to electrolyse one mole of water (H_2O) to split it into its component hydrogen and oxygen gases is;

E/mole = 237,000 Joules   ... A14.4

So, the energy required to electrolyse the annual increase in water in each square metre of seawater would be;

$E/A = 44.3 \times 10^6$ Joules/m²   ... A14.5

The radius of the Earth R = 6,378,000 metres

The surface area of a sphere is $A = 4\pi R^2$ The Earth isn't a perfect sphere but if we assume it's close enough, the surface area would be;-

101

$$A_{EARTH} = 5.11 \times 10^{14} \text{ m}^2 \quad \dots \text{A14.6}$$

About 71% of the Earth's surface is covered by ocean. So the surface area of the sea is;-

$$A_{SEA} = 3.63 \times 10^{14} \text{ m}^2 \quad \dots \text{A14.7}$$

So, from equations A14.5 and A14.7 the total energy required to electrolyse away the total *increase* in seawater levels every year would be;-

$$E_{TOTAL} = 1.61 \times 10^{22} \text{ Joules} \quad \dots \text{A14.8}$$

Appendix 15 – Wind Turbines

Wind turbines provide an effective means of harnessing energy from the atmosphere. The Kinetic Energy of the wind is given by;-

$$KE = \tfrac{1}{2}mv^2 \quad ... A15.1$$

where v is the speed of the wind.

The mass of air passing through a turbine per second is given by;-

$$m/t = v \times A \times \rho_{air} \quad ... A15.2$$

where A is the cross-sectional area of the turbine and ρ_{air} is the density of air.

Combining equations A15.1 and A15.2 we can say the theoretical power P captured by a turbine working at 100% efficiency would be ;-

$$P = 0.5 \times A \times \rho_{air} \times v^3 \quad ... A15.3$$

Large wind turbines have a radius of 40 metres r = 40m and the *average* wind speed is v = 10 m/s

The density of air ρ_{air} = 1.293 kg/m³

Therefore, the theoretical power P produced by a wind turbine comes out to be;

$$P = 3.25 \times 10^6 \text{ W}$$

Most devices of this kind are about 75% efficient, so the expected *useful* power output from each device is;

$$P = 2.44 \text{ Mega Watts} \quad ... A15.4$$

And this, in reality, is the kind of power that is generated from turbines of this kind. In general, they achieve somewhere between 2MW and 3MW.

A standard unit kilowatt-hour of energy in the UK costs on average 24.5 pence to the consumer, so the average wind turbine that produces 2.44 MW-hours delivers on average £597 ($752 US dollars) of electricity every hour at retail prices. A standard wind turbine of this size costs in total about £50,000 ($63,000 US dollars) including installation. This means that the average turbine only has to run for 83.73 hours (about 3.5 days) to pay for itself.

Obviously, the wind doesn't blow everywhere at 10 m/s every day, but *on average* it blows at this speed around the entire globe. If maintained correctly, most turbines last for anything up to 25 years. Various component parts have a much shorter lifespan, such as gear-shafts that might last anything between 5 years and 10 years, but it's easy to see why wind turbines are proving so cost effective at providing clean energy.

Appendix 16 – Wind Turbine Cooling

If we built the 209 million wind turbines, sufficient to capture the 1.61 $\times 10^{22}$ Joules of energy needed to electrolyse the rise in sea-levels every year, we'd also succeed in cooling the atmosphere. Here we calculate the decrease in the temperature of the atmosphere we might expect.

Atmospheric pressure P is given by;

$$P = h \times \rho_{air} \times g \qquad ... \text{A16.1}$$

where h is the equivalent height of the atmosphere, assuming a constant density of air ρ_{air} and g is the acceleration due to gravity, which we'll assume remains constant over these distances.

Rearranging we can say...

$$h = P/ (\rho_{air} \times g) \qquad ... \text{A16.2}$$

The volume of all the air in the atmosphere is V where;-

$$V = A \times h \qquad ... \text{A16.3}$$

where A is the total surface area of the Earth.

The mass of the air in the atmosphere m is given by;

$$m = V \times \rho_{air} \qquad ... \text{A16.4}$$

Therefore, using equations A16.3 and A16.4 we can say ...

$$m = A \times h \times \rho_{air} \qquad ... \text{A16.5}$$

Substituting for h from equation A16.2 we get...

$$m = (A \times P)/g \qquad ... \text{A16.6}$$

The radius of the Earth R = 6,378,000 metres, so assuming the Earth is almost spherical we can say;

$$A = 4\pi R^2 = 5.11 \times 10^{14} \text{ m}^2$$

We know the air pressure P = 101,325 N/m^2 and g = 9.81 m/s^2

Therefore, putting these values into equation A16.6 the estimated mass of our atmosphere is;

$$m = 5.28 \times 10^{18} \text{ kg} \quad \text{... A16.7}$$

If we decrease the heat energy ΔE of a mass m then we get a temperature decrease ΔT depending on the Specific Heat Capacity of the material where;-

$$E = m \times SHC \times \Delta T \quad \text{... A16.8}$$

The Specific Heat Capacity of air is SHC_{AIR} = 993 J/kg Kelvin

Using the value for the energy E = -1.61 x10^{22} Joules we'd need to electrolyse away the rise in sea water every year and the value for the mass of the atmosphere from equation A16.7 we get ...

$$\Delta T = -3.06 \text{ }^\circ c \quad \text{... A16.9}$$

So, in one year, we could in theory remove double the *total* increase in global warming that has occurred over the last two hundred years, during the entire industrial age.

Even if we burned 1/18th (about 6%) of the total hydrogen produced by electrolysis to prevent any rise in sea levels, (the amount that we'd need to burn to meet 100% of the world's current energy needs) we'd still reduce the temperature of the global atmosphere within the space of a single year by more than enough to compensate for the entire increase in global warming of the atmosphere that has ever been caused by human activity.

Obviously, there may be other contributary factors to take into consideration. Both the sea and the land will be acting as major heat sinks that will no doubt yield significant energy to reduce this decrease in temperature to a considerable extent (particularly given the high Specific Heat Capacity of water) but the fact remains, this approach could prove to be a major step forward in controlling the increase in global warming, and as such, it is a solution that should be given appropriate consideration.

Stop The Storms

Appendix 17 – Burning Hydrogen Fuel

Standard water molecules are each made up of one atom of oxygen and two atoms of hydrogen H_2O.

The atomic mass of oxygen is M_O = 16.0 grams/mole

The atomic mass of each hydrogen atom is M_H = 1.00797 grams/mole

So, in any volume of water there are 16 grams of oxygen for every 2 x 1.00797 grams of hydrogen. This means hydrogen only makes up about 11.19% of the weight of water. The annual increase of 3.4 kg of water in each square metre of ocean would therefore contain 0.3763 kg of hydrogen.

When burned, each kilogram of hydrogen releases 120 MJ of energy, so we could expect to get a theoretical maximum of 45,156,160 Joules of energy from the annual sea water rise on each square metre of ocean surface.

With the total surface area of the ocean standing at A = 3.63 x10^{14} m^2 then the total, theoretical maximum energy produced would be 1.64x10^{22} Joules.

The efficiency of energy capture from this kind of process would probably be about 70% so we could realistically expect the *useful* energy produced in this way to be;

$$E = 1.15 \times 10^{22} \text{ Joules.}$$

Currently, the total annual energy consumption of the entire world is 6.34x10^{20} Joules (634 exa-Joules). This means, the hydrogen produced from the electrolysis of rising seawater could potentially produce 18.1 times more energy than the world uses each year and could therefore enable the reliance on fossil fuels to be eliminated.

Stop The Storms

Appendix 18 – Storm Energy Distribution

The velocity of wind V in a storm cyclone typically varies in direct proportion with distance from the centre of the storm r up to a maximum value of V;

$$V = k \times r \quad \text{... A18.1}$$

Where k is an arbitrary value depending on the individual storm. Typically, in a major storm, the maximum value of V might be 60 m/s reached at a distance r = 20 km so in such a case, the value of k would represent the wind velocity increasing up to a value at the rate;

$$k = 60/20000 = 0.0003 = 3 \text{ m/s per km}$$

The kinetic energy of a small slice of the storm of mass dm would be;-

$$KE = \tfrac{1}{2} \, dm \times V^2 \quad \text{... A18.2}$$

Assuming the storm height h remained constant, we could say;-

$$dm = h \times 2\pi r \times dr \times \rho_{air} \quad \text{... A18.3}$$

Where ρ_{air} is the density of air.

Substituting A18.1 and A18.3 into A18.2 gives the total KE of the storm ;-

$$KE = \int \rho_{air} \times \pi \times k^2 \times h \times r^3 \, dr \quad \text{... A18.4}$$

$$KE = [\rho_{air} \times \pi \times k^2 \times h \times r^4]/4 \quad \text{... A18.5}$$

Stop The Storms

The table below illustrates how energy would be distributed in such circumstances.

r1	r2	$r1^4$	$r2^4$	$r1^4 - r2^4$	%
10	9	10000	6561	3439	34.39%
9	8	6561	4096	2465	24.65%
8	7	4096	2401	1695	16.95%
7	6	2401	1296	1105	11.05%
6	5	1296	625	671	6.71%
5	4	625	256	369	3.69%
4	3	256	81	175	1.75%
3	2	81	16	65	0.65%
2	1	16	1	15	0.15%
1	0	1	0	1	0.01%

TOTAL   10000

Table A18.1 – Schematic Energy variation in a storm

Approximately 34% of the total kinetic energy of the storm would exist within about 10% distance of the radius at which maximum wind velocity occurs, assuming the energy distribution beyond the distance at which maximum velocity occurs is broadly similar to the distribution at distances closer to the centre of the storm.

Appendix 19 – Magnet Field Diverts High Velocity Winds

Major cyclones contain large volumes of tiny droplets of water, many of which have a radius r = 10 μm. With a density of about 1,000 kg/m^3 the mass of each of these droplets is about;-

m = 4.19 x 10^{-12} kg

These droplets can carry a charge of about q = 1x10^{-14} Coulombs.

The force on a mass m moving in a circle of radius r is given by;

F = mv^2/r   ... A19.1

The force on a charge q moving at velocity v in a magnetic field B is given by;

F = Bqv   ... A19.2

From A19.1 and A19.2 we can say;

r = mv/Bq   ... A19.3

The magnetic field B at the centre of a coil of radius R with N turns carrying current I and with a core of permeability of $\mu = \mu_r \times \mu_o$ where μ_r is the relative permeability and μ_o is the permeability of free space is given by;

B = μNI/2R   ... A19.4

Using these well-known formulae, it's possible to come up with a wide range of fairly simple design proposals that would act to divert wind flows by varying degrees. The use of a core with high relative permeability might help to limit costs quite considerably. For example, Supermalloy, which is composed of approximately 79% nickel, 16% iron, and 5% molybdenum has a Relative Permeability as high as 1,000,000 or more.

Stop The Storms

On a small scale, a coil of radius R = 1 metre with N = 2,000 turns could be used to deflect rain droplets passing at velocity v = 60 m/s by about 90° with fairly modest running costs.

If copper wire with a radius of 1mm were used to make the coil, its resistance R would be R = 67.23 Ω and the voltage required to drive the device would be 336 volts which would provide a current of 5 Amps, giving a power consumption of about 1.7 kW

This is only a small device that would prove the concept at fairly minimal cost. It would in theory be possible to build much larger scale devices that would prove much more effective over a greater range. However, any such devices would have to be designed to be mobile so that they could be moved in a timely fashion to the best location and made to reach appropriate altitudes to achieve the best possible results.

Appendix 20 – Temperature Rise Near Sun

The power per unit area P/A emitted by a perfect radiator is given by the Stefan-Boltzmann law...

$$P/A = \sigma T^4 \quad ...A20.1$$

where T is the temperature in Kelvin.

The *total* power from the sun remains largely constant at different distances from the sun as there isn't anything much in empty space to block it, however the *power per unit area decreases* at greater distances as the area through which the power travels, increases with distance r...

$$(P/A)_r = P_T/4\pi r^2 \quad ... A20.2$$

where $(P/A)_r$ is the power per unit area at distance r from the sun and P_T is the total power emitted by the sun.

If we assume the Earth acts like a perfect radiator and emits as much energy as it receives then A20.1 and A20.2 =>

$$T_2/T_1 = (r_1/r_2)^{1/2} \quad ... A20.3$$

where T_1 is the temperature at distance r_1 and T_2 is the temperature at r_2.

If we wish to calculate the temperature of the Earth at a point r_2 half the current distance r_1 from the sun then $r_2 = 0.5 \times r_1$

$$T_2 = T_1 \times 2^{0.5} \quad ...A20.4$$

The average temperature on the surface of the Earth is about 14°c which is about 287 Kelvin. So, if the distance to the sun halved the temperature would increase to 406 Kelvin which is about 133°c well above the 100°c S.T.P. boiling point of water.

Stop The Storms

Appendix 21 – Falling Moon

Consider the scenario that the moon has suffered a major collision with a meteor that has caused it to lose all its orbital Kinetic Energy, causing it to fall to the Earth's surface.

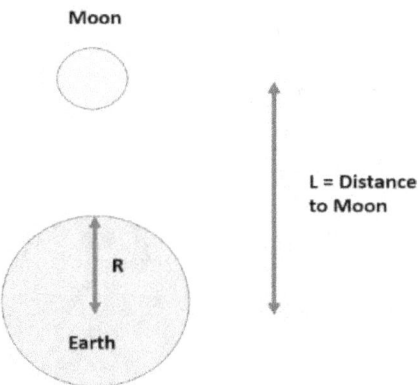

Diagram A21.1 – The Moon Falls to Earth

The diagram above shows the Earth with radius R and the moon at distance L. If the moon fell to Earth, it would lose Potential Energy which would convert to Kinetic Energy, causing it to speed up as it fell. The Kinetic Energy KE the moon would attain is given by...

$$KE = 1/2 M_{moon} V_{moon}^2 \quad ... A21.1$$

where M_{moon} is the mass of the moon and V_{moon} is the maximum velocity it would achieve immediately before impact with the Earth.

The change in Potential Energy of the falling moon would be given by;

$$\Delta PE = GM_{EARTH} M_{MOON}(1/R - 1/L) \quad ... A21.2$$

where G is Newton's Gravitational constant, M_{EARTH} is the mass of the Earth, R is the radius of the Earth and L is the starting distance between the Earth and the moon.

Stop The Storms

Since the gain in KE of the falling moon is equal to its loss in PE we can say...

$$V_{moon}^2 = 2\,GM_{EARTH}\,(1/R - 1/L) \quad ... A21.3$$

The average distance between the Earth and the moon is;

L = 384,400,000 metres

The radius of the Earth is;-

$R = 6.38 \times 10^6$ metres

The mass of the Earth is;-

$M_{EARTH} = 5.97 \times 10^{24}$ kg

and Newton's Gravitational constant $G = 6.6733 \times 10^{-11}\,Nm^2kg^{-2}$

Putting these values into equation A21.3 gives an estimate for the velocity the moon would have reached immediately before it crashed into the surface of the Earth;-

$V_{moon} = 11,084$ m/s

The plane of the orbit of the moon around the Earth makes an angle of about 5.14 degrees with the plane of the orbit of the Earth around the sun. Although the moon does at times briefly cross the path of the Earth, it's unlikely the moon would make a full head-on collision with Earth. But we're looking to calculate the worst-case scenario here, so let's assume a direct head-on collision does occur. Because of the law of conservation of linear momentum, we can say...

$$M_{EARTH} \times V_{EARTH} - M_{MOON} \times V_{MOON} = M_C \times V_1 \quad ... A21.4$$

where M_C is the combined mass of the Moon and Earth (assuming they coalesce) and V_1 is their new combined velocity.

The mass of the moon $M_{MOON} = 7.35 \times 10^{22}$ kg.

118

Putting the known values into equation A21.4 gives an estimate of their resulting velocity V_1

$$V_1 = 29,300 \text{ m/s}$$

i.e. the Earth would have lost about $\Delta V_{EARTH} = -486$ m/s

Assuming this reduced velocity is not sufficient to maintain the combined mass of the Earth and moon in a stable orbit at distance r_1 from the sun, the combined mass would fall in towards the sun to a new stable orbit, distance r_2 from the sun. This fall would cause the loss of some of its Potential Energy, which would be converted to an increased Kinetic Energy and a new orbital velocity V_2.

The new Kinetic Energy would be;-

$$KE_2 = \tfrac{1}{2} M_c V_2^2 = 1/2 M_c V_1^2 + GEM_c(1/r_2 - 1/r_1) \quad \dots \text{A21.5}$$

where E is the mass of the sun.

We can simplify equation A21.5 to give …

$$V_2^2 - V_1^2 = 2GE(1/r_2 - 1/r_1) \quad \dots \text{A21.6}$$

If the orbit at distance r_2 can be assumed to be circular, we can say the centripetal force F_c is given by;-

$$F_c = M_c V_2^2/r_2 = GEM_c/r_2^2 \quad \dots \text{A21.7}$$

Therefore…

$$r_2 = GE/V_2^2 \quad \dots \text{A21.8}$$

Substituting from equation A21.8 into equation A21.6 gives…

$$V_2^2 = 2GE/r_1 - V_1^2 \quad \dots \text{A21.9}$$

Putting in the values for V_1 = 29,300 m/s and r_1 = 1.496 x10^{11} metres gives;-

V_2 = 30,300 m/s

Putting this value into equation A21.8 gives...

r_2 = 1.45 x10^{11} metres

From appendix A20 and equation A20.3 we determined ...

$T_2/T_1 = (r_1/r_2)^{1/2}$ ... A21.10

The average ambient temperature on Earth is about 14°c i.e. T_1 = 287.16 Kelvin. Putting values for r_1 and r_2 into this equation gives a value for T_2...

T_2 = 291.84 Kelvin i.e. 18.68 °c

This represents an increase in the Earth's temperature of some 4.68°c

Appendix 22 – Overhead Powerlines

The National Grid operate over 7,000 km of high voltage overhead powerlines in the U.K.[49] These powerlines typically operate at temperatures between 30°c and 90°c.

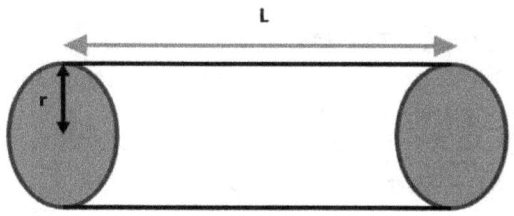

Diagram A22.1 – Cylindrical Power Cable
Power cable length L and radius r.

If we assume an average operating temperature for a high voltage overhead cable to be about 60°c then this equates to a temperature of 333.16 Kelvin.

The total outer surface area A of a cable of length L and radius r is given by;-

$$A = 2\pi r \times L \quad \text{... A22.1}$$

Typically, high voltage power cables have a radius of at least 2cm or 0.02m

Over 7,000 km this gives a total surface area of;-

$$A = 879,646 \text{ m}^2 \quad \text{... A22.2}$$

The total power per unit area emitted by an object at temperature T measured in Kelvin is given by Stefan-Boltzmann law...

$$P/A = \sigma T^4 \quad \text{... A22.3}$$

where σ is the Stefan constant $\sigma = 5.669 \times 10^{-8}$ Wm^{-2}K^{-4}

Putting the value for T = 343.16 Kelvin and A = 879,646 m^2 into equation A22.3 we can estimate the power loss from our high voltage overhead powerlines P as;

$$P = 6.14 \times 10^8 \text{ Watts}$$

The average home in the U.K. uses about 10kW-hours of energy per day. This equates to a *constant* consumption of about 417 Watts (which is about one third of the energy consumed each day by the average home in the USA)

Therefore, the estimated loss of power from overhead high voltage powerlines in the U.K. would be sufficient to power about 1.5 million homes. If correct, this represents a considerable loss given that we are thought to have less than 30 million homes in total.

Appendix 23 – Aluminium v Copper

Some powerlines are manufactured out of copper but aluminium is used to manufacture a significant percentage of high voltage powerlines. It's interesting to compare the performance of aluminium against copper to highlight some of the important differences.

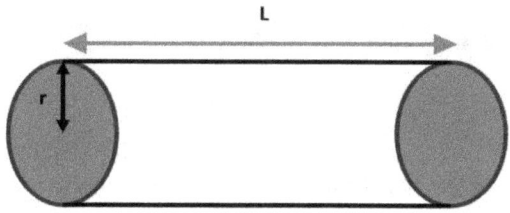

Diagram A23.1 – Power Cable

Power cable length L and radius r.

The resistance R of a length of cable L is;-

$$R = \rho_r \times L/A_x \qquad ... A23.1$$

where ρ_r is the resistivity of the material, L is the length of the cable and A_x is the cross-sectional area.

Assuming a *circular* cross-section then we can say;-

$$A_x = \pi r^2 \qquad ... A23.2$$

where r is the radius of the cable.

If we have two pieces of cable of the same length L say 1 metre, one made of copper and one made of aluminium, then to get the same resistance R we can say...

$$\rho_{CU} \times L/A_{CU} = \rho_{AL} \times L/A_{AL} \qquad ... A23.3$$

Where ρ_{CU} is the electrical resistivity of copper and ρ_{AL} is the resistivity of aluminium and A_{CU} is the cross-sectional area of a copper cable and A_{AL} is the cross-sectional area of the aluminium cable.

We can simplify this to..

$$A_{AL}/A_{CU} = \rho_{AL}/\rho_{cu} \qquad ...A23.4$$

The resistivity of aluminium ρ_{AL} = 2.65 x 10^{-8} Ωm

The resistivity of copper ρ_{CU} = 1.7 x 10^{-8} Ωm

So, to get the *same resistance* over the same length L of cable the cross-sectional area of the aluminium would need to be 1.56 times greater. i.e. the *radius* of the aluminium cable would need to be 1.25 times greater than the copper cable.

The densities of these two materials differs greatly.

The density of aluminium is d_{AL} = 2,710 kg/m³
The density of copper is d_{CU} = 8,930 kg/m³

This means a block of copper would be 3.295 heavier than a block of aluminium of the *exact same dimensions*.

However, since the *cross-sectional area* of the copper cable would only be 64.2% of the area for the aluminium cable, then the weight of copper required would only be 2.11 more than the weight of an aluminium cable with the exact same electrical resistance. This though is quite a significant difference and one that should not be ignored as there are considerable engineering and mechanical challenges to be considered when constructing supports (pylons) in the construction of overhead power transmission lines.

The price of metals fluctuates more or less every second of every day, and prices of individual materials can change rapidly, depending on supply and demand which is often driven by technological advances.

Currently a metric tonne (1,000 kg) of copper and aluminium is priced as follows;-

Copper => £5,700 per tonne
Aluminium => £2,950 per tonne

This makes each kilogram of copper 1.93 times more expensive than a kilogram of aluminium. Overall then, taking into account the greater mass of the copper required, the price of copper cables is about 4.08 times the price of aluminium cables to achieve a powerline with the exact same electrical resistance.

In addition, the thinner copper cables would have the disadvantage of running at a higher temperature as they'd have a smaller radius and less surface area from which to radiate the equivalent loss of power.

According to the Stefan-Boltzmann equation...

$$P/A = \sigma T^4 \quad \text{... A23.5}$$

where P/A is the power radiated *per square metre* from an object with temperature T measured in Kelvins.

Consider for example a typical aluminium cable running at 60°c (333.16 Kelvin). A copper cable with the exact same electrical resistance and therefore with a radius of only 80% of the aluminium cable, would only have 0.8 of the surface area A_s over the same length considering $A_s = 2\pi r \times L$

This means the value of the term T^4 for copper would be 1.25 times higher than for aluminium for the same power emitted with the exact same electrical resistance and electrical current. Therefore, the copper cable would run at 352.16 Kelvin (79°c) whilst conducting the same power and achieving the same power loss, compared to the thicker aluminium cable with the exact same electrical resistance running at 60°c.

Stop The Storms

From Wein's displacement law, the wavelength λ_{max} at which the highest amount of energy is emitted is given by;-

$$\lambda_{max} \times T = K_{WEIN} \quad \ldots A23.6$$

where T is the temperature in Kelvin and K_{WEIN} is Wein's constant where K_{WEIN} = 2.90 x 10^{-3} mK

Therefore, an aluminium cable running at 60°c (333.16 Kelvin) emits the highest amount of its energy at wavelength...

$$\lambda_{AL} = 8.64 \ \mu m$$

Whereas the thinner copper cable with the same electrical resistance running 20°c hotter at 79°c (352.16 Kelvin) with the same total power loss would emit the highest amount of its energy at wavelength...

$$\lambda_{CU} = 8.17 \ \mu m$$

Sulphur dioxide has an absorption band at 8.7 μm (infrared radiation produced most strongly by a perfect radiator running at 330.8 Kelvin) so in this particular case, if aluminium cables were running at 60°c (333.16 Kelvin) then copper would be a much preferable choice to reduce energy absorption by this greenhouse gas, even though it would be running at the higher temperature of 79°c (352.16 Kelvin).

The thermal coefficient of resistance for aluminium is α = 40 x 10^{-4} K^{-1} and for copper α = 39 x 10^{-4} K^{-1} where the resistance R_T at some temperature T_2 is ;

$$R_T = R_0(1 + \alpha\Delta T) \quad \ldots A23.7$$

where R_0 is the resistance at temperature T_1 and $\Delta T = T_2 - T_1$

We can see that for a larger temperature increase of say 100°c (i.e. ΔT = 100 this value has been chosen simply for convenience) the increase in the resistance of a piece of copper wire would be 39% whilst the increase in the resistance of an aluminium cable *subject to the same temperature increase* would be a very similar 40%

So, there is no significant difference between them in terms of the variation in electrical resistance *when running at the same temperature*. However, since copper would run 20°c hotter than an aluminium cable with the *same initial resistance*, starting say at 0°c then the resistance of the copper *at its operational temperature* would be about 8% higher than the aluminium cable, so we could expect a *total loss of power* of 0.54% with copper as opposed to 0.50% for aluminium.

This is a significant difference when one considers this *difference* would meet the total energy requirements of 11,600 UK homes but a price probably worth paying given that it would significantly reduce the greenhouse energy absorbed by sulphur dioxide.

Stop The Storms

Appendix 24 – Powerlines Increase Global Warming

The area of land which comprises the U.K. is $A = 2.43 \times 10^{11}$ m^2
The volume V of air above the U.K. can be calculated from;

$$V = h \times A \qquad \text{... A24.1}$$

where h is the height of the atmosphere.

The air pressure P on the surface of Earth is given by;

$$P = h \times \rho \times g \qquad \text{... A24.2}$$

where ρ is the average density of air and g is the acceleration due to gravity.

The mass of air m above the U.K. is given by;-

$$m = V \times \rho \qquad \text{... A24.3}$$

Equations A24.1 & A24.3 =>

$$m = h \times A \times \rho \qquad \text{... A24.4}$$

Re-arranging equation A24.2 =>

$$h \times \rho = P/g \qquad \text{... A24.5}$$

Putting this in equation A24.4 =>

$$m = A \times P/g \qquad \text{... A24.6}$$

Putting in values;-

$$A = 2.43 \times 10^{11} \text{ m}^2$$

$$g = 9.81 \text{ m/s}^2$$

$P = 101{,}325 \ N/m^2$

This comes out to be …

$m = 2.50 \ x \ 10^{15} \ kg$

This is an estimate of the mass of air standing above the U.K.

The increase in temperature ΔT caused by an input of energy E into a substance with Specific Heat Capacity SHC is given by;-

$E = m \ x \ SHC \ x \ \Delta T$ … A24.7

The Specific Heat Capacity SHC of air is;-

$SHC = 1{,}005 \ J/kg \ x \ K$

The amount of energy transmitted via Overhead Powerlines in the U.K. annually is $9.32 \ x 10^{17}$ Joules.

 With a loss rate of about 5% this means *currently* the amount of energy E radiated into the atmosphere by Overhead Powerlines in the U.K. is;

$E = 4.66 \ x \ 10^{16}$ Joules

Putting these values into equation A24.7 we get an annual temperature increase ΔT of…

$\Delta T = 0.0185^{\circ}c$ per year

Over 50 years this would amount to a temperature increase of;

$\Delta T_{(50 \ YEARS)} = 0.93^{\circ}c$

 This would be the increase in global temperature caused by Overhead Powerlines in a period of 50 years if the entire surface of the globe suffered the same loss of energy from Overhead Powerlines.

Only 29.2% of the surface of the globe is covered by land. So, if every corner of the world had the same energy losses as the U.K. we could expect an increase in the temperature of the atmosphere of 0.27°c at *current* rates of energy loss.

However, it's already planned that the amount of energy transmitted in the U.K. by Overhead Powerlines will be doubled in the next decade.[50][51]

This means that at these elevated levels of energy transmission, the increase in the atmospheric temperature caused by Overhead Powerlines over a 50 year timescale is estimated to be;

$$\Delta T = 0.54°c$$

This estimate is based on the assumption that all the energy lost by powerlines is absorbed by the atmosphere which of course is not likely to happen, so the actual temperature increase may be lower than this value. It also assumes all the loss of energy goes into the atmosphere. In truth, some of this energy will also be absorbed by the land and the sea.

Furthermore, it assumes everywhere in the world has similar levels of energy loss from powerlines as the U.K. which may or may not be true. However, it also doesn't take into account any *further increase* in energy loss from powerlines caused by further increases in energy transmitted beyond what is already planned for the next ten years.

0.54°c may sound like a small increase in global temperature but in truth it could prove to be *catastrophic* given our current precarious position caused by the failure to date to bring the increase in global warming under control.

Stop The Storms

References

1. "Carbon dioxide now more than 50% higher than pre-industrial levels".
https://www.noaa.gov/news-release/carbon-dioxide-now-more-than-50-higher-than-pre-industrial-levels
National Oceanic and Atmospheric Administration.
Accessed 15th November 2024.

2. NASA
https://climate.nasa.gov/vital-signs/sea-level/
Sea Level | Vital Signs – Climate Change: Vital Signs of the Planet
Accessed 14th November 2024

3. Matthews, J.B.R.; Möller, V.; van Diemenn, R.; Fuglesvedt, J.R.; et al. (9 August 2021). "Annex VII: Glossary". In Masson-Delmotte, Valérie; Zhai, Panmao; Pirani, Anna; Connors, Sarah L.; Péan, Clotilde; et al. (eds.). *Climate Change 2021: The Physical Science Basis. Contribution of Working Group I to the Sixth Assessment Report of the Intergovernmental Panel on Climate Change* (PDF). IPCC / Cambridge University Press. pp. 2215 - 2256.
doi:10.1017/9781009157896.022.
ISBN 9781009157896.

4. NASA
The Atmosphere: Getting a Handle on Carbon Dioxide - NASA Science
https://science.nasa.gov/earth/climate-change/greenhouse-gases/the-atmosphere-getting-a-handle-on-carbon-dioxide/
Accessed 14th November 2024

5. The World Counts
Global-CO2-Emissions
https://www.theworldcounts.com/challenges/climate-change/global-warming/global-co2-emissions
Accessed 15th November 2024

6. Metoffice UK
Clouds
https://www.metoffice.gov.uk/weather/learn-about/weather/types-of-weather/clouds
Accessed 15th November 2024

7. University Corporation for Atmospheric Research | University Corporation for Atmospheric Research
Size of Raindrops and Cloud Droplets
https://scied.ucar.edu/image/aerosols-raindrop-cloud-droplets-sizes
Accessed 15th November 2024

8. Optics and Lasers in Engineering Volume 32, Issue 5, November 1999, Pages 419-435 – "Reflectance measurements of aluminium surfaces using integrating spheres"
I Lindseth, A Bardal, R Spooren.

9. Ecological Indicators Volume 146, February 2023, 109905 "Water surface albedo and its driving factors on the turbid lakes of Northeast China"
Jia Du, Pierre-Andre Jacinthe, Kaishan Song, Haohao Zhou

10. "After Great Hurricane of 1896".
http://www.wdl.org/en/item/4032/
World Digital Library.
Accessed 16th Nov 2024

11. Wikipedia
Hurricane Helene - Wikipedia
https://en.wikipedia.org/wiki/Hurricane_Helene
Accessed 12th November 2024

12. Atlantic Oceanographic and Meteorological Laboratory
NOAA's Atlantic Oceanographic & Meteorological Laboratory
https://www.aoml.noaa.gov/
Accessed 15th November 2024

13. "Mount Mitchell, North Carolina"
Peakbagger.com
Accessed 15th November 2024

14. Great Pyramid of Giza - Wikipedia
https://en.wikipedia.org/wiki/Great_Pyramid_of_Giza
Accessed 15th November 2024

15. Burj Khalifa - Wikipedia
https://en.wikipedia.org/wiki/Burj_Khalifa
Accessed 15th November 2024

16. Florida - Wikipedia
https://en.wikipedia.org/wiki/Florida
Accessed 15th November 2024

17. "General Facts about the Gulf of Mexico"
GulfBase.org. 6th Oct 2024.
Accessed 14th November 2024

18. Weather – April 2013, Vol 68, No4 "The Greenhouse Effect and Carbon Dioxide"
Weyi Zhong and Joanna D. Haigh Dept Physics and Grantham Institute for Climate Change, Imperial College London

19. Sincere thanks to the 'South Florida Water Management District' for help in kindly providing an overview of the desalination and water supply operation in around the South Florida region.
Desalination | South Florida Water Management District
https://www.sfwmd.gov/our-work/alternative-water-supply/desalination
Accessed 16th Nov 2024

20. "Definitions of the SI base units". physics.nist.gov.
29th May 2019.
Accessed 8th November 2024.

21. Chihuahuan Desert - Wikipedia
https://en.wikipedia.org/wiki/Chihuahuan_Desert
Accessed 16th November 2024.

22. UK Enhanced Weathering | The University of Sheffield
https://www.sheffield.ac.uk/uk-enhanced-weathering/our-research
Accessed 19th November 2024

23. Agri-climate report 2022 - GOV.UK
https://www.gov.uk/government/statistics/agri-climate-report-2022/agri-climate-report-2022

24. Calcium - Wikipedia
https://en.wikipedia.org/wiki/Calcium
Accessed 19th November 2024

25. DeMore, W. B., et al. (1997). "Chemical kinetics and photochemical data for use in stratospheric modeling" (Jet Propulsion Laboratory, Publication 97-4). This document is a comprehensive compilation of data on the absorption cross-sections of atmospheric gases, including N_2O. It mentions the strong absorption of N_2O in the UV region, including wavelengths around 203 nm, where it dissociates primarily into nitrogen (N_2) and oxygen (O) atoms.

26. Johnston, H. S. (1976). "Nitrous Oxide and Nitric Oxide Photodissociation." This paper also covers the absorption of UV light by N_2O, and the dissociation at various wavelengths, including the important region around 203 nm.

27. Action CO2 Warming. Climate Change – The Facts UK Met Office 2009
Booklet outlining details of impact from warming of climate.

28. Science Data Book – R.M. Tennent, Oliver & Boyd, Open University 1971
ISBN 0 05 002487 6

29. NASA's Earth Observatory: https://earthobservatory.nasa.gov
https://earthobservatory.nasa.gov/
Accessed 28th November 2024

30. NOAA's National Centers for Environmental Information (NCEI):
https://www.ncei.noaa.gov
https://www.ncei.noaa.gov
Accessed 28th November 2024

31. 'Thunderstorms and Lightning' by S.A. Rutledge and B. H. H.
Christian. In the book *Severe Convective Storms*, American
Meteorological Society, 1994.

32. 'The electrical structure of thunderstorms' by M. P. Sturrock et
al., published in *Reviews of Geophysics*, 1994.

33. U.S. National Weather Service (NWS) – According to the NWS, the
typical electrical charge in a thundercloud is on the order of **10-100
coulombs**. This is the charge needed to produce the voltage
differences that lead to lightning discharges. (National Weather
Service, "Thunderstorms and Lightning," NOAA, available from:
https://www.weather.gov)

34. National Severe Storms Laboratory (NSSL) – The NSSL mentions
that the amount of charge in a thundercloud is typically around 20 to
100 coulombs. They also discuss how this charge separation leads to
lightning strikes. (National Severe Storms Laboratory,
"Thunderstorms," available from: https://www.nssl.noaa.gov)

35. 'Thunderstorm and Lightning' by Vernon Cooray (2010), the
electrical charge within a typical thundercloud is cited to range
between 10 to 100 coulombs.

36. Measurement of the Electrical Properties of a Thundercloud Through Muon Imaging by the GRAPES-3 Experiment
B. Hariharan, A. Chandra, S. R. Dugad, S. K. Gupta, P. Jagadeesan, A. Jain, P. K. Mohanty, S. D. Morris, and P. K. Nayak et al. (GRAPES-3 Collaboration)
Phys. Rev. Lett. 122, 105101 – Published 15 March, 2019
DOI: https://doi.org/10.1103/PhysRevLett.122.105101

37. The Resistivity Of Water Explained | Atlas Scientific
https://atlas-scientific.com/blog/resistivity-of-water/
Accessed 2nd December 2024

38. Cloud seeding - Wikipedia
https://en.wikipedia.org/wiki/Cloud_seeding
Accessed 11th December 2024

39. Boiling Point Calculator
https://www.calctool.org/thermodynamics/boiling-point
Accessed 17th December 2024

40. Holland (1980) Model
Holland, G. J. (1980). *An Analytical Model of the Wind and Pressure Profiles in Hurricanes. Monthly Weather Review*, 108(8), 1212–1218.
DOI: 10.1175/1520-0493(1980)108<1212:AAMOTW>2.0.CO;2

41. Willoughby et al. (2006)
Willoughby, H. E., Darling, R. W. R., & Rahn, M. E. (2006). *Parametric Representation of the Primary Hurricane Vortex. Part I: Observations and Evaluation of the Holland (1980) Model. Monthly Weather Review*, 134(4), 1102–1120.
DOI: 10.1175/MWR3107.1

42. NOAA Hurricane Research Division (HRD)
https://www.aoml.noaa.gov/hrd
Data sets and visualizations of wind speed profiles.
Accessed 23/12/2024

43. The Chicxulub Asteroid Impact and Mass Extinction at the Cretaceous-Paleogene Boundary
Peter Schulte , Laia Alegret, Ignacio Arenillas, José A. Arz, Penny J. Barton, Paul R. Bown, Timothy J. Bralower, Gail Christeson, Philippe Claeys, [...], and Pi S. Willumsen+ 31 authors & affiliations
Science
5 Mar 2010
Vol 327, Issue 5970
pp. 1214-1218
DOI: 10.1126/science.1177265

44. A revision of the formation conditions of the Vredefort crater.
Allen, N. H., Nakajima, M., Wünnemann,K., Helhoski, S., & Trail, D. (2022). Journal of Geophysical Research: Planets, 127, e2022JE007186.
https://doi.org/10.1029/2022JE007186

45. Journal of Geophysical Research: Planets
Volume 127, Issue 8 e2022JE007186
Research Article
Open Access

46. Assessments of the energy, mass and size of the Chicxulub Impactor
Hector Javier Durand-Manterola, Guadalupe Cordero-Tercero
arXiv:1403.6391 [astro-ph.EP]
(or arXiv:1403.6391v1 [astroph.EP]
https://doi.org/10.48550/arXiv.1403.6391

47. Space Encyclopedia – Heather Couper & Nigel Henbest, Dorling Kindersley Books 2008
ISBN 978-1-4053-3531-7

48. Top 10 hottest places on Earth 2025 | BBC Science Focus Magazine
https://www.sciencefocus.com/planet-earth/hottest-place-on-earth
Accessed 20th Jan 2025

49. Substations, pylons and overhead lines | National Grid ET
https://www.nationalgrid.com/electricity-transmission/who-we-are/running-our-network/substations-pylons-and-overhead-lines?
Accessed 20th January 2025

50. Electric Home+1The Guardian+1
https://electrichome.uk/news/national-grid-outlines-a-record-35bn-investment-to-nearly-double-uk-electricity-transmission-capacity-by-2031
Accessed 2nd April 2025

Over the next decade, the UK's electricity transmission capacity is projected to nearly double, driven by significant investments aimed at modernizing the grid and integrating renewable energy sources.

National Grid has announced plans to invest £35 billion by 2031 to upgrade the UK's electricity infrastructure, which includes the construction of new pylons, cables, and substations.

51. https://www.bbc.co.uk/news/articles/c207113jz73o
The National Energy System Operator (NESO) has indicated that approximately 1,000 miles (1,600 kilometres) of new overhead power lines will be required to meet the government's clean energy targets by 2030.
Accessed 2nd April 2025

52. R. M. Tennent Science Data Book 1971 Oliver & Boyd ISBN 0 05 002487 6

P.J. Naughton

Stop The Storms

P.J. Naughton

* Various personal opinions, general discussion points, estimated dimensions and physical constants have also been presented in this work for which no reference is available. Much of this information is widely available across the public domain and in various discussion forums and blogs which deal with matters of climate-change. Although precise details vary according to the exact source, an attempt has been made to present the values and opinions thought to be most widely accepted at the present time. No doubt, improved definition of some of these points will be achieved over time and will likely be further clarified and amended as further progress is made in our understanding of climate related issues.

In some cases, values for various parameters have been rounded and some facts have been summarised for brevity or for the purposes of simplification. This work contains a number of estimates which are used to form a basis for general discussion.

This is not intended to be a strictly precise scientific work. Although the author has attempted to avoid misleading anyone who might choose to access this text, none of the details quoted should be relied on for any purposes whatsoever. All the facts contained herein, including all the calculations shown and the conclusions reached, should all be independently verified before being utilised in any way whatsoever.

*** THE END***